Get in Touch with Your Spirit

Other Books

By

Brian

Beyond Your Pale

Getting Past Me And Being Closer To Thee

Think For Yourself Control Your Life

See Thru Other People And Know Yourself

Breakup Recovery A New Beginning

The Can Do Spiritual Exercises

I'm Dying To Get To Heaven

Peace Of Mind

Isight

ISBN

978-1-737 2228-6-6

Get in Touch with Your Spirit

119 Positive Spiritual Messages and Affirmations

Each one of us has a spirit
So
This book is for everyone

Brian Thomas

THE PURPOSE AND GOAL

THE PURPOSE OF THIS BOOK IS TO HELP
SOMEONE IN SOMEWAY IF THIS BOOK I ABLE
TO HELP ONLY **ONE** PERSON IN SOMEWAY
IT WILL HAVE ACHIEVED OUR GOAL.

Table of Contents

Introduction

God, you created me for what I do not know

I can only believe and have faith you will show

Me what I am here for and by what means

I am to fulfill my purpose, no matter what it seems

To be and no matter what you have deemed to be

My life is now in your hands

Now and forever in the sands

Of time my life will never be my own

I'm only here on this earth as but a loan

Of part of your spirit and soul

You made me, you created me, and discarded the mould

You created me, for what is not known

I can only hope that I will be shown

One day when you will tell me in your way

Until that day comes, I will continue to serve and pray

Nothing to Fear

Day by day in each and every way, I'm getting better and better, stronger and stronger, through the grace of God.

The people who have had death experiences come back to life with wonderful tales of what it was like on the other side. They speak of a happiness and bliss which is beyond our imagination. Too good to be true, so to speak. Most people have a fear of death, and a fear of the unknown. This is normal since our basic instinct is survival. Death can be a little scarier if we have led a negative, selfish life, which claimed many victims of our greed and lust. It's hard to believe that we will be forgiven no matter what we did.

There was a hypnotist who could hypnotize himself and cease all bodily functions. When he would do this, he would have three MDs present and all would declare him dead. He was never asked what it was like on the other side. I guess they felt that it was too personal of a question to ask, but one day a young man asked him this question: "What about death?"

The hypnotist looked him straight in the eye, paused a second or two, and said, "There is nothing to be afraid of." He didn't know what the young man had done in the past or would do in the future. There were no ifs, ands or buts, just "There is nothing to fear." If we can get in this mindset, life will become more meaningful.

All things come from God. Thank you God for loving and forgiving me. Thank you God for your mercy. I love you dear God.

A Small Miracle

Day by day in each and every way, I'm getting better and better, stronger and stronger, through the grace of God.

Dave was a neurotic kleptomaniac. He was insulting to most people. He was Jewish, was a success, and made a fortune. He lost it all, including his family. This is why he became the way he was. He stole, he lied, and had to insult people, mostly Gentiles, but he was a great salesman. He ran out of people and companies to scam. The only work he could find was to be a counselor, AKA, a watch dog at a juvenile delinquent home.

The counselor was in charge of a house, which was home to about 20 inmates. They were all from the ghetto, under 18, and were charged with crimes from petty theft to murder. No one was able to reach these kids, except Dave. He somehow earned not only their respect but their love. They all called him Mr. Dave and would go out of their way to do as he asked. None of the other counselors even came close to having that kind of rapport. These kids felt that place changed people. I don't know what he did or how he did it. Maybe he accepted them as they were and showed them in some way that he cared about them. I don't know, but what I do know, is that a small miracle took place. Maybe if we look for the best in people, those people will find it in themselves.

All things come from God. Thank you God for loving and forgiving me. Thank you God for your mercy. I love you dear God.

Mike

Day by day in each and every way, I'm getting better and better, stronger and stronger, through the grace of God.

Mike was a man's man, both in stature and demeanor. He served in the Marines during WWII and survived Guadalcanal. He was generous to a fault and had a special type of kindness. He came back home and married the love of his life. Things were good until one day he came home early and found his best friend, the one he had let stay in his home, in bed with his wife. Something called care left him. He became hard, with no feelings. His uncle, who was connected to organized crime, got him a job as a collector for a loan shark. He broke bones and smashed faces without giving it a thought. He did this for many years and rose in rank in the organization. He was on his way to the top when he found out he had Uremia, poisoning of the blood with urine, and the doctor gave him six months to live. Thinking he would be dead in six months, he took a tour around the world for six months. He came back. He didn't die, but he did run into a girl who he had dated for a short while a long time ago. Long story short, he fell in love and was able to love someone again. He was happier than anytime he had been in his life. He didn't want to die and he called a friend up feeling sorry for himself. His friend said to him, "Mike, you've always lived like a man, and now you're going to have to die like a man." Mike died like a man. He died with great love in his heart, in his last days. You see its never too late to find true love and have that love till your last breath.

All things come from God. Thank you God for loving and forgiving me. Thank you God for your mercy. I love you dear God.

A Mom's Place

Day by day in each and every way, I'm getting better and better, stronger and stronger, through the grace of God.

Mothers have an awful responsibility. They can determine the outcome of the lives that they gave birth to or the ones that were put in their care for one reason or another. They have to teach these children so many things for them to have a good and productive life. They not only have to teach, they have to be an example for them. They have to be strong, honest, patient. The list goes on, but you get the idea.

There comes a time in their life where their children or child begins to make their own decisions. Hopefully, all that the mother has tried to instill will pay off and the children will turn out good. There is one lesson or idea that needs to be repeated time after time. The children or child needs to be informed that they have a purpose in the life they live. They may not know then what that purpose is. The fact is they have one and there's no avoiding it. It's like a finger-

18

print, everyone has one and it's different than anyone else's. So many people have absolutely no idea they have a very special purpose. They go through their life not even knowing they have one. Mom or dad or anyone, teach these children they have a purpose.

All things come from God. Thank you God for loving and forgiving me. Thank you God for your mercy. I love you dear God.

Goodwill

Day by day in each and every way, I'm getting better and better, stronger and stronger, through the grace of God.

The word God comes from the word good, as in God is good. Goodwill is the will of God, which is primarily kindness. We are admonished to spread goodwill wherever we go and whatever we do. But do we do that? It's not hard to do. We have countless exchanges with other people in our everyday life. Some of these exchanges are problems. Sometimes others cause us unnecessary problems due to their "don't care" attitude or incompetence.

For example, a phone number is provided if you have a problem. You have been greatly inconvenienced by someone else's doing. You are angry or put out so you call the number. The one thing to remember is that the person who answers the phone did not cause your problem. Now is the time to adopt an attitude of kindness. Spread some goodwill. The person you got on the phone probably has to deal with angry people all day long. A little bit of kindness will go a long way in getting your problem resolved. You have just spread some goodwill and your world and the world is just a little bit better off. Kindness pays big dividends.

All things come from God. Thank you God for loving and forgiving me. Thank you God for your mercy. I love you dear God.

Candid

Day by day in each and every way, I'm getting better and better, stronger and stronger, through the grace of God.

What does it take to be candid? In a word, honest. Is it possible to be candid in every situation? In a word, no. You cannot be candid with everyone because candid means truthfulness and not everyone wants to hear the truth or what you believe to be true. They only want to hear what they want to and what gives them a feeling of satisfaction. It is also good to remember that what you think to be true is not true. You believe you are being candid, but you may be wrong. You have to be very close and know the person well enough to be candid and even then, you have to be careful of that person's feelings. If you are one of those people who are candid with people and about situations, there is a piece of you missing. That piece is consideration.

All things come from God. Thank you God for loving and forgiving me. Thank you God for your mercy. I love

you dear God.

Friendly

Day by day in each and every way, I'm getting better and better, stronger and stronger, through the grace of God.

Want to get along better with people? Want to improve your relations? It's simple. Ask how they are doing. Ask what's going on in their life Ask what they are doing this weekend. Ask if they have plans to go anywhere soon. Have you got the drift? Well, if you haven't, the point is talk about them instead of yourself. Let your conversation be about them. They will appreciate the fact that someone cares about them and what they are doing. Put yourself aside. I'm sure your ego is big enough to handle that, and if it isn't, maybe you should stop and think about someone other than yourself. You will be surprised at how good you will make other people feel and the bonus is you will feel better about yourself.

All things come from God. Thank you God for loving and forgiving me. Thank you God for your mercy. I love you dear God.

Calm

Day by day in each and every way, I'm getting better and better, stronger and stronger, through the grace of God.

What's the big deal about being calm? The big deal is most people do not stay calm when bad things happen between people, even the ones we love or when terrible events take place in our life. Most of us do not have the self-discipline to remain calm. We become irritated, frustrated, and even violent. All of these things make the matter worse. It's not easy to stay calm in the worst of situations or even when small problems inevitably come up. Our life is always going to be a life of problems. No way to avoid it. We can however minimize the situation by telling ourselves to be calm no matter what happens. I know. Easier said than done, but it is possible to do, and when we do, things are not as bad as they seem.

All things come from God. Thank you God for loving and forgiving me. Thank you God for your mercy. I love you dear God.

Silence

Day by day in each and every way, I'm getting better and better, stronger and stronger, through the grace of God.

When life confronts you with overwhelming problems, you can retreat in your own mind and try to conjure up a positive attitude to deal with everything facing you. This will always be a benefit and will help in many ways. The best path to getting a positive is to go someplace quiet where there is an absence of noise. There you can take advantage of the benefits of silence. When you are silent, let your mind relax. Thoughts will come to you since they have a clear path. The silence will allow you to look at things differently. There will be some solutions you may not have thought of before or you might just gain total acceptance of the situation, which will leave you in peace. Silence can be the key.

All things come from God. Thank you God for loving and forgiving me. Thank you God for your mercy. I love you dear God.

Love of God

Day by day in each and every way, I'm getting better and better, stronger and stronger, through the grace of God.

We are physical, mental, and spiritual people. Should we choose to be a more spiritual person, we have to arrive at a certain conclusion. The first is that there is a God. Second, we believe that there is a God. Third, to be truly spiritual, we must love God more than we love the world and the things of the world. We must love this God more than we love ourselves. We can try to love God more than the world. We can feel it in our minds that we love God more than the world, and we can love the world and the things of the world a lot less, but in the end we will still love the world. We are humans and have a human nature. The same holds true of ourselves. We can put ourselves aside more than usual, but we cannot stop caring and loving ourselves or liking ourselves. The very best that we can do is to develop a mindset which says and means it, "I love you God." I thank you God for everything I know, all things come from you and be thankful for God's mercy. We can make a choice to be a spiritual person, but the price is too high to be a 100% spiritual person because we are still human.

All things come from God. Thank you God for loving and forgiving me. Thank you God for your mercy. I love you dear God.

Dad

Day by day in each and every way, I'm getting better and better, stronger and stronger, through the grace of God.

Dear Dad,

I'm just writing to tell you how much I appreciate you teaching me all of the different things that have helped me in so many ways. I can't thank you enough for all of your encouragement, especially in my time of need. You were always there when I needed you. I drew from your strength and learned to be strong through your example. Thank you, dad, for all you have given and done for me. I wish you could read this letter, but you died when I was ten-years-old. I never even got to know you, but I believe you would have been all of the above.

If you happen to be in your forties, fifties, or sixties, and you still have your father, would it be such a bad idea if you

Dad

were to sit down and write him a letter, thanking him for all he has done for you and given you? You owe him that much and both of you will feel better and best yet, you will find yourself closer than you have ever been before. If you are inclined to do this, remember tomorrow is guaranteed to no one.

All things come from God. Thank you God for loving and forgiving me. Thank you God for your mercy. I love you dear God.

Besides You

Day by day in each and every way, I'm getting better and better, stronger and stronger, through the grace of God.

When you first begin to have a conversation over the phone or in person (forget texting), the first thing you may ask is how they are. Then you put yourself aside. You can ask how their weekend was, what did they do? This can be followed up by what are you doing this week, how's the family and what are you up to? Then, you can ask about their health and how they feel. Are you beginning to get the drift of this? You are talking about them and what they did and their interests. You have put yourself aside. You have dropped the big "I" from the conversation. When you get off the phone, they will feel good, but you'll feel even better. If they start to direct the conversation back toward you, make the answers short and direct the conversation back to them. This applies to anyone you are talking to even the person making the appointments or returning an order or placing an order.

31

Besides You

Your life will go smoother and your spirit will be happier and more peaceful.

All things come from God. Thank you God for loving and forgiving me. Thank you God for your mercy. I love you dear God.

I F

Day by day in each and every way, I'm getting better and better, stronger and stronger, through the grace of God.

Your thoughts will always be upward, outward, and away from yourself. You will always enjoy wonderful physical, mental, emotional, and spiritual strength and wellbeing, developing into the conviction and authority of joy and spiritual understanding that will be a reflection of beauty, harmony, and truth shown to you uniquely through God, by the way of subconscious logic, deduction, and inherent intuition, if you choose it to be.

All things come from God. Thank you God for loving and forgiving me. Thank you God for your mercy. I love you dear God.

I'll Never Forget You God

Day by day in each and every way, I'm getting better and better, stronger and stronger, through the grace of God.

As our life comes toward its end
Our minds begin to lose something
Then start to blend past with present
Forgetting much of what was
The thoughts we allow to stay with us
No matter what comes into our life,
We make a vow to never forget the ones
We love and cherish as we grow old
But most of all, we'll never be told
That we forgot God because we'll promise,
"I'll never forget you God"

No matter how much my memory dims

How could I ever forget you after all you have done

I'll Never Forget You God

You gave me life and let me live under your sun
You were there when I needed you
You were there when I was happy and when I was blue
You knew my heart and were forgiving
Of all my sins and all my sinful living, too

How could I ever forget you?
When only you were the one who knew
The things that held my deepest regrets
And you were the one who forgave me of my debts
I'll never forget you God, this I vow
I make this promise to you here and now

All things come from God. Thank you God for loving and forgiving me. Thank you God for your mercy. I love you dear God.

Feel Good

Day by day in each and every way, I'm getting better and better, stronger and stronger, through the grace of God.

What is the bottom line of all human behavior? It's almost too simple to be true. The bottom line on all human behavior and everything, and I mean everything, is to feel good. We do what we do no matter what that is, to feel good. It may be something very negative, but if it didn't make us feel good to do it, we would not have done it. It could also be positive and extravagant, like donating more money to a charity or giving someone money when we really didn't have to give it to them.

Our spiritual side will do things that make other people feel good. A smile, a kind word, a compliment, an inquiry as to how they are doing or how they are feeing are but a few examples of things we can do to make others feel good. The big bonus is that when we do this, we will feel not only good, we will feel better and the Best part is it doesn't cost us any money or effort to accomplish a lot of these things.

All things come from God. Thank you God for loving and forgiving me. Thank you God for your mercy. I love you dear God.

Hell

Day by day in each and every way, I'm getting better and better, stronger and stronger, through the grace of God.

Hell is said to be "Fire and Brimstone." If this is for wayward souls, it won't have the least bit of effect on them since they are spirits and not subject to physical pain. Fire and brimstone are physical elements of this world. They would no have effect in the world of the spirits. God is known for his unconditional love, and a God of vengeance would be a stark contradiction. If there is to be harm for turning against God, then hell would be confined to the spirit. A definition of hell could be that when you die, you come before God and experience his love, which produces a happiness beyond your wildest dreams. If you have turned your back on God and lived for the joys of the world, you could be consigned to a space in the universe where there is no soul except yours. You would be saddled with the thought of being alone with only yourself and not having the greatest joy and happiness you had experienced ever for an of eternity. No end. This would be hell.

All things come from God. Thank you God for loving and forgiving me. Thank you God for your mercy. I love you dear God.

True Love is Never a Loss

Day by day in each and every way, I'm getting better and better, stronger and stronger, through the grace of God.

Sometimes our loss can be a gain
If a positive attitude you do maintain
You can think back to all of your love
And be so happy that your loved one is now above
You can look back at the good times you had
And the things you did together will make your heart glad
That you found each other and became of one heart
And know that in a way you will never be apart
So by now you have went on to discover
That after your loved one there can be no other
And that one day you can look forward to being
    together again
And through the love of God on that you can depend

True Love is Never a Loss

All things come from God. Thank you God for loving and forgiving me. Thank you God for your mercy. I love you dear God.

Socrates

Day by day in each and every way, I'm getting better and better, stronger and stronger, through the grace of God.

Socrates was convinced of the immortality of the soul. He believed that this was the core of man's being and that nothing else made any sense in the grand scheme of things. He projected that for man to achieve harmony, he must first be virtuous. He must be just, honest, and have the courage to do what is right. He believed that unless man believed in the immortality of his own soul, there was little or no reason to lead a life of virtue, which in turn leads to harmony with his fellow man.

A man who does not believe in the immortality of the soul will turn to a life of vice since there is nothing after death, then one must enjoy life to the fullest even at the expense of others. This produces a world of disharmony, conflict, and confusion. Socrates looked forward to his death for he believed that the soul would come into the presence of the great good and would live forever in a state of harmony and bliss.

All things come from God. Thank you God for loving and forgiving me. Thank you God for your mercy. I love you dear God.

Have

Day by day in each and every way, I'm getting better and better, stronger and stronger, through the grace of God.

The word "have" is one of strongest, if not the strongest, words in our language. If you look in the dictionary, it has many different meanings. The meaning which stands out above all others is something you must do, you have no choice. When you apply that meaning to something that you want such as "I have to get a new coat," you have given that task top priority above others things. When you use the word in regards to yourself or others, such as you have to do this or else. Or else what? When someone places a demand on you such as you have to perform one kind of act or another, it pushes you into making a choice that you may not want to do. Most of the time it is yourself that says that to yourself. Actually, there is only one thing you have to do. That is to die. You have to die. All of the other haves in your life are a matter of choice, one way or the other. The next

Have

time you say I "have" to do this or have to do that remember you have a choice no matter how important it is, you still only have one thing you "have" to do.

All things come from God. Thank you God for loving and forgiving me. Thank you God for your mercy. I love you dear God.

When They
Were Happy

Day by day in each and every way, I'm getting better and better, stronger and stronger, through the grace of God.

I saw them when they were at their best
I try to forget all of the rest
Memories resurface of when they'd fight
Usually over something so slight
And despite the way they'd go after each other
They were all I had, my father and mother

It was all a blur, how both would shout
And to this day, I'm not sure what about
They called each other unpleasant names,
Since of course both of them were to blame
I loved them both, but the fighting I would hate
And of course, thoughts came much too late

When They Were Happy

To tell them how much they meant to me
It was something that was not meant to be

They died early, before I could say
Now regret fills my heart each day,
But I recall past weekends, how they searched
For antique bargains like kids at play,
Hours on end, seeking out treasure
Their happiness was beyond measure

Too much of our time is spent fighting over meaningless worldly matter and things; we forget what's really important and what has a true meaning in our life. We are human, we all do this, but we don't have to. We can choose to act with love and kindness or react with anger and fury. God gave us that choice.

All things come from God. Thank you God for loving and forgiving me. Thank you God for your mercy. I love you dear God.

Always the Best

Day by day in each and every way, I'm getting better and better, stronger and stronger, through the grace of God.

Things work out for the best. How many times have we heard that? A lot of times it may seem that things do not work out for the best, especially on our end. The problem is that a lot of times they don't work out immediately. There are factors involved. For something to work out for the best, it may take several or many events to happen before the final action. It may even take years or decades or even centuries for the best to happen. We cannot know God's plan. We just don't understand when things don't happen in our favor right away. They may seem to work out for the worst. We have no idea of the chain of events that it will take for things to come out for the best or the time involved. Since we don't know that, this is where faith, becomes necessary. Blind faith in some cases. It is necessary for you to believe that things work out for the best, not to know how they do.

49

Always the Best

All things come from God. Thank you God for loving and forgiving me. Thank you God for your mercy. I love you dear God.

A Thing

Day by day in each and every way, I'm getting better and better, stronger and stronger, through the grace of God.

You can own, possess, cherish and use a thing. A thing being something inanimate. You cannot love a thing. You may like it, adore it, relish it, enjoy it, or even be dependent on it. You cannot however love a thing. You can only love something that has a spirit like God, or any and all of his children. Love is a very special thing. When a man meets and becomes involved with a woman and vice versa, our second strongest instinct comes into play. Sexual desire. The hormones begin to rage and take over. It is then that we begin to look at the person as a sexual thing. Something we can use to fulfill our desire. We may like or even have a feeling of love for the person, but love will usually take second place. Those of you who wish to become more spiritual will put love first. Your goal will be to see that the other person has more pleasure and enjoyment than you. You will find a way to put yourself aside and concentrate on giving that person the ultimate excitement and pleasure that will satisfy their sexual desire instead of yours. Make no mistake you will have satisfaction also, but you will be giving the other person the gift of a lifetime. They will feel pure love instead of feeling like a thing that has just been used.

All things come from God. Thank you God for loving and forgiving me. Thank you God for your mercy. I love you dear God.

Unconditional Love

Day by day in each and every way, I'm getting better and better, stronger and stronger, through the grace of God.

Most love has conditions put on it. If someone you love does something that hurts you, anger will probably be the response. When a person says something that makes you feel bad or inadequate, most people will return the insult. There are always going to be areas of conflict with other people. Most of the time we respond with emotions, usually negative. Unconditional love is continuing to show that person or persons love no matter what they may say or no matter what they may do. Unconditional love is putting all the other emotions aside except love. The first step toward having unconditional love is to believe we are better than no one. Different but not better. This allows us to have love in our hearts for everyone. Unconditional love is looking past what people have done and are still doing and still have love in your heart. When we choose to forgive other people, we can take it one step further by saying it never happened. Choosing to love and love unconditionally will put us in close touch with our spiritual side.

All things come from God. Thank you God for loving and forgiving me. Thank you God for your mercy. I love you dear God.

Oneness

Day by day in each and every way, I'm getting better and better, stronger and stronger, through the grace of God.

Oneness is a state where a person is not plagued by internal conflicts or guilt. An internal conflict will divide a person's being. If a person is torn between making a living and being there for his family, this is an example of an internal conflict. It leaves the person divided and not knowing what to do. Feelings of guilt prevail if he doesn't do his job and on the other hand if he neglects his family. Oneness is where a person is able to have a life where there is little or no division or a conflict internally. There will always be external conflict, but if a person can find a balance and concentrate on one issue at a time, their life will be more harmonious. Oneness is a wholeness of personality where all parts of a person's personality are in agreement. His wants, needs, and desires are in harmony with his temperament and talents. His behavior is compatible with what he values and what

Oneness

is important to him. He keeps himself together by keeping his thoughts together. He pursues one thing at one time in unison and spirit.

All things come from God. Thank you God for loving and forgiving me. Thank you God for your mercy. I love you dear God.

Character

Day by day in each and every way, I'm getting better and better, stronger and stronger, through the grace of God.

Character is formed when a person overcomes their natural inclinations. These include following the line of least resistance or taking the easy way out. This also includes giving in to personal pleasures and wants at the expense of others and avoiding that which is unpleasant by procrastination. Those who have character value what is right over what is good for them. They have principles and will not compromise these at any price. They are true to themselves and what they stand for. Their lives are guided by their morals and their behavior reflects this. They realize that their strength of character is their most important asset. What they value most is not physical, material, or of this world. Their true values are of a spiritual nature.

All things come from God. Thank you God for loving and forgiving me. Thank you God for your mercy. I love

you dear God.

Endurance

Day by day in each and every way, I'm getting better and better, stronger and stronger, through the grace of God.

No matter how bad things are, we will prevail if we persevere and continue. Endurance is key to living our life to its fullest, regardless of the conflict and stress which will always be produced by this world in which we live. The key we are all caught in the middle of forces beyond our control. These forces include nature, other people, and even ourselves. Bad and terrible things can and will happen to us. It's the nature of the material world. God created the physical world, which can only exist through opposing forces. The greatest gift God gave besides life is the capacity to endure what we must in this physical world. Our power to endure comes from God and our own spirit.

All things come from God. Thank you God for loving and forgiving me. Thank you God for your mercy. I love you dear God.

Its of the World

Day by day in each and every way, I'm getting better and better, stronger and stronger, through the grace of God.

Should you wish to become a more spiritual person, then you must put away some worldly things. We are both spiritual and worldly at the same time. We all have worldly needs but it's a matter of degree. There are times when you will be buying something and the product is out of stock and won't be in for several weeks. Instead of fretting about you not being able to get what you want when you want it, you can take the spiritual approach and say to yourself, "Its only of the world." You are basically saying worldly things should not matter as much as they do. When it comes to the choice of a Cadillac or Ford, again, "its only of the world." Settling for less importance on worldly things and realizing in the end they do not matter, will allow you to become a more spiritual person if in fact that is your desire. If you choose to be a more worldly person, then that becomes your desire. You have a choice, now or forever more.

All things come from God. Thank you God for loving and forgiving me. Thank you God for your mercy. I love you dear God.

Talking About Others

Day by day in each and every way, I'm getting better and better, stronger and stronger, through the grace of God.

When we talk about others, it usually refers to something negative about those people. This can be taken another way. When most people speak with others, they usually begin by talking about themselves. They are so absorbed in themselves, their interests, and what they're doing or have done or are planning to do, that it will most likely dominate the conversation. Their point of view is so important to them, there is no room for another's. We might find it a great deal more interesting if we would bring the other person into the conversation by asking about them, what they are doing, what they are planning to do, rather than gear the conversation about ourselves. We would feel better that we had taken an interest in other people and their lives and made them feel good about themselves, especially if they happen to be on the shy or introverted side. You will feel better and they will feel better, too. They will feel closer to you. It's very worldly to think only of yourself and your importance. True humbleness can be a very spiritual thing. We are more likely to be remembered for what we did for others and how we made them feel rather than what we did.

All things come from God. Thank you God for loving and forgiving me. Thank you God for your mercy. I love you dear God.

Positive Connection

Day by day in each and every way, I'm getting better and better, stronger and stronger, through the grace of God.

We are all introverts, extroverts, or something between the two. We do not have to be an extrovert to extend ourselves to others, but it does help. Anyone can extend themselves to anyone at any time. The biggest reason for doing this is that it will make you feel better about yourself. There is always something about any person that you can make a positive comment about. For instance, if a person is all sweaty and dirty, a positive comment could be, "You look like you're having a hard day." If an older person is having a hard time opening the door, offer to lend them a hand. Should a woman be carrying a colorful purse, you can always comment on what a beautiful purse that is. When you do this, you have made a positive connection with another person. You can change the course of a person's day with just a casual comment. Who knows, you may make a new friend. Small talk makes you feel good and hopefully the other person will feel better too. Two people who never met and a little small talk brings out two smiles, positive feelings, and a spiritual connection is worth far more than things or money. Two spirits have come together.

All things come from God. Thank you God for loving and forgiving me. Thank you God for your mercy. I love you dear God.

Transformation

Day by day in each and every way, I'm getting better and better, stronger and stronger, through the grace of God.

Transformation in a human is not rare, but it is far from common. The reason probably lies in the fact that people are controlled more or less by their habits and are conditioned in certain ways as to cause the mind to be set in one place where it eventually stays. This is called a mindset and is a powerful thing for the individual. Transformation requires a break in established habits or behavioral patterns. Transformation is usually adopting a mode of behavior which is totally opposite of the present behavior. A transformation is sometimes the product of an epiphany coupled with a tremendous desire for a better life. A graphic visualization of what this new life will be like will enhance the inclination to change. A spiritual awakening along with faith can be the key to a complete transformation. A better life is around the corner.

Transformation

All things come from God. Thank you God for loving and forgiving me. Thank you God for your mercy. I love you dear God.

Joyfulness

Day by day in each and every way, I'm getting better and better, stronger and stronger, through the grace of God.

Joyfulness begins in the heart, as in, "they have joy in their heart." How does one fill his or her heart with joy so they may have joyfulness or become full of joy? It all starts with the thoughts we think. Our only true choice in life is the thoughts we think. If we think positive, happy thoughts, then that is the first step in a joyful heart. Next, is finding out what brings you joy and doing it as a job or hobby, even as a pastime. We must also come out of ourselves to achieve selflessness. A selfish heart can never be a joyful heart. And last but not least is extending yourself to others so you may touch their lives, even in a very small way. The act of giving and knowing you have touched someone's life will help bring about a joyful heart. Those who lead a life of joy can be identified by their attitude and facial expressions. They radiate joy unlike others who pretend to be joyful, but are

Joyfulness

really only wearing it as a costume. Joyful souls have a firm connectedness to the power of God and it shows.

All things come from God. Thank you God for loving and forgiving me. Thank you God for your mercy. I love you dear God.

Dying

Day by day in each and every way, I'm getting better and better, stronger and stronger, through the grace of God.

The minute we are born, we begin to die. We enter into a world of opposition and proposition which are conflicting forces. These forces begin to attack our body immediately. They are bent on our physical destruction. Their purpose is to dispose of us and eventually they do. Everyone dies.

It takes less than four minutes after you die for the onset of decomposition to begin. The physical world sets out to reduce you to dust and it will succeed. Eventually, you will be returned to the earth in the form of molecular grams. The good news is that your soul is impervious to this process. Your soul is eternal. If you are reading this, you are still alive. The big question is what are you going to do with the time you have before you die? You do have a choice. You can become more worldly or you can become more spiritual. Your spirit is alive, always will be. God works through your spirit, so the more spiritual you become, the closer you are to God. You can become more spiritual; the choice is yours.

All things come from God. Thank you God for loving and forgiving me. Thank you God for your mercy. I love you dear God.

Reverence

Day by day in each and every way, I'm getting better and better, stronger and stronger, through the grace of God.

Reverence is a form of absolute respect. It goes beyond respect and crosses over into a state of awe and even perhaps love. A person who has reverence has a profound regard for that which they consider sacred and beyond their reach as a human being. A reverent person has achieved a state of humility where they put something above themselves that is whatever they revere. This will most likely involve something of a spiritual nature. A reverence for the spiritual acknowledges a higher power than what exists on earth. A spirited reverence recognizes that what is on earth is finite, and what exists in the spirited realm is infinite. A person who is reverent has a deep respect for the life God gave them and the infinite mercy and goodness of God.

All things come from God. Thank you God for loving and forgiving me. Thank you God for your mercy. I love

you dear God.

No One Sees

Day by day in each and every way, I'm getting better and better, stronger and stronger, through the grace of God.

True humility is accepting and believing we are better than no one. We may be different, but we are no better. This allows us to have love in our heart for everyone and be free of judgment and critical behavior. We can be like the man who never met a stranger. It allows us to reach out to anybody and everybody with a kind word, a compliment, or a little encouragement. When you do this, there will be times when people seem to be into themselves. When you extend yourself to someone like that, you may see something in them that no one else sees. You can touch the heart of someone who is ignored by most people. You may be able to change a life with a few kind words and some encouragement. You never know how far the ripples go when you throw a rock into a body of water and the best part is it doesn't cost you anything to do it. If you are a spiritual kind of person, God has reached out and touched you. Now it's your turn.

All things come from God. Thank you God for loving and forgiving me. Thank you God for your mercy. I love you dear God.

Karma

Day by day in each and every way, I'm getting better and better, stronger and stronger, through the grace of God.

Karma is a law of nature which states for every action, there is an equal reaction. It's just physics. This definitely holds true in the physical world, but what about the spiritual world? The soul is impervious to harm, or is it? God is a God of pure unconditional love. Your soul comes from God and maybe it's a part of God. This we do not know. We can only believe. If you do not believe in or ignore God, will God ignore you when you come before God on judgement day. The day of your worldly death? If the soul is infinite, as believed, then how will God deal with this? We don't know. We only know and believe God is a God of unconditional love. That is a love that no matter what you do or say, you are still loved. Should this be true, then any punishment would come into conflict with pure unconditional love. Then the

Karma

law of karma would not apply to our soul. This may or may not be true. We will know the day we die.

All things come from God. Thank you God for loving and forgiving me. Thank you God for your mercy. I love you dear God.

What Are Your Trying to Get Out of This World

Day by day in each and every way, I'm getting better and better, stronger and stronger, through the grace of God.

We were born into this world for a very short period of time. The world has everything of a physical nature to offer you. You have the choice of what you want to take or get out of this world. Do you want to get all the pleasure you can, usually at the expense of others? Do you want to get all the things and money you can? If you can't get enough of things, pleasure, and money and always want more, you have become a greedy, worldly person. If on the other hand, you choose to put yourself aside and extend yourself to others you will have achieved true humility. If you are somewhere in the middle as most people are, then you probably have a balanced life. In all of the above you are trying to get something from this world for the short time you are in it. The thing to remember is that no matter what you choose to get out of this world, is that you have a spirit, which never dies. Your spirit needs peace of mind, recognition, joy, and true happiness. This is something the world can't give you. You must find it within yourself.

All things come from God. Thank you God for loving and forgiving me. Thank you God for your mercy. I love you dear God.

We are Nothing and Everything

Day by day in each and every way, I'm getting better and better, stronger and stronger, through the grace of God.

We came from nothing, just two microscopic cells which developed and evolved into the most complex mechanism on the face of the earth. We began to die the minute we were born. The decay process was set in motion and eventually we will die and decay into the smallest particle on earth, the atom. This is why we are nothing. We were all born with a spirit, which will never die, and a purpose, whatever that may be. Our spirit is our most precious possession because it is everything. It is infinite and is our connection to God. It will guide us if we let it. This is why we are everything.

All things come from God. Thank you God for loving and forgiving me. Thank you God for your mercy. I love you dear God.

Small Talk

Day by day in each and every way, I'm getting better and better, stronger and stronger, through the grace of God.

We are all introverts, extroverts, or something between the two. We do not have to be an extrovert to extend ourselves to others, but it does help. Anyone can extend themselves to anyone at any time. The biggest reason for doing this is that it will make you feel better about yourself. There is always something about any person that you can make a positive comment about. For instance, if a person is all sweaty and dirty, a positive comment could be, "You look like you're having a hard day." If an older person is having a hard time opening the door, offer to lend them a hand. Should a woman be carrying a colorful purse, you can always comment on what a beautiful purse that is. When you do this, you have made a positive connection with another person. You can change the course of a person's day with just a casual comment. Who knows, you may make a new friend. Small talk

Small Talk

makes you feel good and hopefully the other person will feel better too. Two people who never met and a little small talk brings out two smiles, positive feelings, and a spiritual connection is worth far more than things or money. Two spirits have come together.

All things come from God. Thank you God for loving and forgiving me. Thank you God for your mercy. I love you dear God.

All of Us

Day by day in each and every way, I'm getting better and better, stronger and stronger, through the grace of God.

This book is written for everyone because everyone has a soul, and just as the body needs nourishment, the spirit also needs some spiritual nourishment, especially those who are in "low spirits." Hopefully this little book will not only give you that nourishment, but a positive feeling about your life and yourself. We are all destined to go to another world, the spirit world. This book does not presume to know what is on the other side, but it would seem that if your spirit is filled with the love of God, love for others, and kindness of heart, there will be a big plus on the other side.

All things come from God. Thank you God for loving and forgiving me. Thank you God for your mercy. I love you dear God.

Spiritual View

Day by day in each and every way, I'm getting better and better, stronger and stronger, through the grace of God.

A way to become more spiritual is to look at things in a spiritual light. Everything that happens to you has a lesson in it. Some lessons are simple; such as if you cross the street against the light and get hit by a car, the lesson is don't cross the street against the light. Should you become discouraged and depressed because all things are going wrong, then the lesson may be that you are going against your spiritual nature and relying on the things of the world to solve your problems. This lesson is to look inside of you to find the real cause of your problem. Your spirit will speak to you if you listen.

All things come from God. Thank you God for loving and forgiving me. Thank you God for your mercy. I love you dear God.

Spirit Care

Day by day in each and every way, I'm getting better and better, stronger and stronger, through the grace of God.

You must take care of your body if you are to maintain good health. It probably never dawns on most of us that we have to take care of our souls, also. This begs the question, how do we take care of our soul? One of the ways we can enhance our soul is communication. When you are communicating with other people, you can focus in on them. Talk about what they are doing, how they feel; in other words, forget yourself and talk about them. Another way is to extend yourself to other people, even the ones you don't know. We should also concentrate on thanking God every day for all we have and for all he's done for us, for loving and forgiving us. Don't forget to thank God several times a day. Spend your time thanking God instead of constantly asking God for so much. When you talk to God, you are speaking to God through your soul. Think less of yourself and more of God. Try to develop a true humility and try to think less of yourself and less of this world. These are just a few of the things that will help you care for your soul. Everything comes from God, especially ideas so if you desire to become more spirited, God will give you some ideas.

All things come from God. Thank you God for loving and forgiving me. Thank you God for your mercy. I love you dear God.

Our Past

Day by day in each and every way, I'm getting better and better, stronger and stronger, through the grace of God.

We all have a past as well as a present and future. We live in the present, but our past can and does influence our present. Our soul, as well as our mind, contains our past for better or for worse. We have all heard the expression "soulful lament" meaning that what has happened to us or what we have done has gone to our very soul. Our soul cries out to us in times like this. We can't erase the past, but we can speak to our soul with acts of love. It's hard for us to forgive ourselves. The mind seems to hold on to regret. Our soul doesn't. Our soul only knows the present. Our soul thrives on love. This is why extending ourselves in love is so important. It's the best thing we can do for body and soul.

All things come from God. Thank you God for loving and forgiving me. Thank you God for your mercy. I love you dear God.

One of the Hardest Things

Day by day in each and every way, I'm getting better and better, stronger and stronger, through the grace of God.

The biggest obstacle that stands in the way of a person becoming spirited is their pride. It is also the hardest thing they will ever overcome. Our pride is connected to our survival instinct, which is our strongest instinct and permeates our body and mind. Every atom in our body is wired to survive and sends that message to our brain, which sends it to our mind. One of the hardest conclusions to arrive at is that we are no better than anyone else on the face of the earth. We may be different and we are, but we are no better. True humility will let us extend ourself to others and thereby become more spirited. Becoming more spirited is the endgame.

All things come from God. Thank you God for loving and forgiving me. Thank you God for your mercy. I love

you dear God.

Look into Their Souls

Day by day in each and every way, I'm getting better and better, stronger and stronger, through the grace of God.

You can look into the souls of others to a degree. Their actions, attitude, and words can tell you a great deal about the condition of their soul or spirit. When you are with someone, think about what's going on with them spiritually. Look past what they are saying or doing and into the reason, the real reason, of their behavior. What they are saying or doing affects their spirit. We can give our own spirit a boost if we can relate to others on a spiritual basis.

All things come from God. Thank you God for loving and forgiving me. Thank you God for your mercy. I love you dear God.

You'll Feel Better

Day by day in each and every way, I'm getting better and better, stronger and stronger, through the grace of God.

The key to understanding human behavior is to be aware of the basic reason that people do what they do. Simply put, people do what makes them feel good. It's as simple as that. Whether it's bad or good, they do it to make themselves feel good or better. When we can put the things and pleasures of the world aside, or have less importance in our lives, we can reduce a great deal of stress, anxiety, and pressure in our life. Once we have done this, and can turn our attention to more spiritual objectives, such as giving encouragement to others, maintaining a positive cheerful attitude and achieve a degree of humility, THEN we realize and believe we are better than no one, we will feel better about ourselves and our life.

All things come from God. Thank you God for loving and forgiving me. Thank you God for your mercy. I love you dear God.

Spiritual Wisdom

Day by day in each and every way, I'm getting better and better, stronger and stronger, through the grace of God.

Everyone has a conscience. Our conscience will tell us if we are doing something which is wrong or negative. We may choose to ignore it and do as we please. We have a choice. Even the worst around us has a conscience. They may try to turn it off and have it so low that they don't hear it, but it's there. Your spirit has the wisdom of the ages built into it. Your soul will speak to you when your spirit means more to you than the things of the world.

All things come from God. Thank you God for loving and forgiving me. Thank you God for your mercy. I love you dear God.

What God Has in Store

Day by day in each and every way, I'm getting better and better, stronger and stronger, through the grace of God.

What God has in store can only be imagined. It cannot be known while we are living, only when we die. We can believe that God is a God of love and we will come into the presence of a love that we cannot even imagine. We will be accepted unconditionally with a love that transcends all others, and it will be eternal. We must believe there is a God or everything is meaningless. Should we choose to put God in our life, only then can we believe but still not know that eternal bliss awaits us.

All things come from God. Thank you God for loving and forgiving me. Thank you God for your mercy. I love you dear God.

Soul Care

Day by day in each and every way, I'm getting better and better, stronger and stronger, through the grace of God.

You must take care of your body if you are to maintain good health. It probably never dawns on most of us that we have to take care of our souls, also. This begs the question, how do we take care of our soul? One of the ways we can enhance our soul is communication. When you are communicating with other people, you can focus in on them. Talk about what they are doing, how they feel; in other words, forget yourself and talk about them. Another way is to extend yourself to other people, even the ones you don't know. We should also concentrate on thanking God every day for all we have and for all he's done for us, for loving and forgiving us. Don't forget to thank God several times a day. Spend your time thanking God instead of constantly asking God for so much. When you talk to God, you are speaking to God through your soul. Think less of yourself and more of God. Try to develop a true humility and try to think less of yourself and less of this world. These are just a few of the things that will help you care for your soul. Everything comes from God, especially ideas so if you desire to become more spiritual, God will give you some ideas.

All things come from God. Thank you God for loving and forgiving me. Thank you God for your mercy. I love you dear God.

Making Money

Day by day in each and every way, I'm getting better and better, stronger and stronger, through the grace of God.

Two men were having a discussion of how much money they were making. A third man said to them, "neither one of you are making any money unless you are printing it yourself. You don't make money. You take money." All the money you have is taken from someone else. There usually is an exchange of goods or services for this before you take the money. What are you willing to do to take the money? How hard are you willing to work? How much money will it take to satisfy you? Are you the kind of person who can never get enough money? If you can never get enough, then you are a greedy person. This not only applies to money, it applies to everything, pleasure and/or things. Greedy people are never happy because they are going down a road which has no end. Greed is the biggest asset of the conman. There must be some greed in order to be conned. A desire for something for nothing. A bold and brazen conman was famous for telling his victims that they were going to be had. He would say, "Right now I have the experience and you have the money; after this is all over, I will have the money and you will have the experience." The victim would laugh. He thought it was funny. It wasn't. Your spirit doesn't need money. It has no use for it. Your spirit needs you and the attention you give to it. Talk with your spirit, it's listening. Listen to your spirit and it speaking to you, and remember, the old saying, "shrouds have no pockets."

All things come from God. Thank you God for loving and forgiving me. Thank you God for your mercy. I love you dear God.

Encourage Others

Day by day in each and every way, I'm getting better and better, stronger and stronger, through the grace of God.

Everyone at one time or another needs some encouragement. When you choose to be a more spiritual person, you become more sensitive to others. You will be able to tell if they are in a situation where they need some encouragement. When you are a spiritual type of person, this is like finding a gold mine. This gives you an opportunity to provide encouragement when it is most needed; you might change the outcome of a person's life or future with your encouragement. Never pass up the opportunity to encourage someone. It will make both of you feel better and accomplish a greater good than you can ever imagine.

All things come from God. Thank you God for loving and forgiving me. Thank you God for your mercy. I love you dear God.

What is a Soul Worth

Day by day in each and every way, I'm getting better and better, stronger and stronger, through the grace of God.

Preachers of all religions like to say they are in the business of saving souls. Money into the millions is given to save souls. What does it take to save a soul? Can words save a soul? Words can make you think, but is that enough to save a soul? What is a soul worth? A soul is priceless. A soul can only be saved by the person it belongs to. When something happens to a person or as a person does something that causes them to realize that the worth of their soul is priceless, only then will their soul be saved.

All things come from God. Thank you God for loving and forgiving me. Thank you God for your mercy. I love you dear God.

Make Every Minute Count

Day by day in each and every way, I'm getting better and better, stronger and stronger, through the grace of God.

All of us have so many years, days, hours, minutes, and seconds to live. No one knows how many minutes they have left. The truth be known, we all waste time. The time we waste is gone forever. So this begs the question, what can be done in a minute? What can you do in a minute to make it count forever? You can give a simple compliment to someone at the checkout line. You can give a smile and say "have a good day" to someone who looks like they need a little cheer. You can open the door for someone. You can help someone who is having a problem lifting something. All of the above takes less than a minute, but look what you have done. You have made someone's day a little brighter when maybe they really needed it and it didn't cost you anything but less than a minute of your time. You will feel good and you will have given your spirit a little boost.

P.S. take a minute each day and thank God for what was given and done for you and for the love and forgiveness you have been granted.

All things come from God. Thank you God for loving and forgiving me. Thank you God for your mercy. I love you dear God.

God is the Only Infinite Reality

Day by day in each and every way, I'm getting better and better, stronger and stronger, through the grace of God.

You're a soldier. You're in a battle. Bullets are zinging past you. The guy next to you takes a bullet to the head. At that moment in time the only force you can turn to is God. There is an old saying, "there are no atheists in foxholes." You become a believer. The world around us is our reality, but it is a finite reality. Everything we can see or touch is disintegrating, and one day will no longer exist. It is finite. On the other hand, what we cannot see or feel or touch is God, which is infinite. The best part of us is our spirit, which we cannot see, feel or touch, and is infinite. We all have the capacity to become more worldly or more spiritual.

All things come from God. Thank you God for loving and forgiving me. Thank you God for your mercy. I love

you dear God.

Consequences

Day by day in each and every way, I'm getting better and better, stronger and stronger, through the grace of God.

There are consequences for everything we do. Some good, some bad. They may come right away or it may take years, but they will come and some are lasting. Here is a true example of this. A beautiful, sensitive woman fell in love and married a man who had been in prison. She gained an insight into what happens to a young man in prison. They had a daughter who she loved dearly, but she always wanted to have a son. She finally got her wish about 10 years later. She adored her son, needless to say the sun rose and set in him. She was so proud of him and let people know it. He graduated from high school and went into the workplace. He became involved with some people who had a plan to make money illegally. Her son was in on it. They got caught. The police came to the house and took her son away in handcuffs in front of the whole neighborhood. She was totally

Consequences

humiliated, but more importantly, devastated. Her heart was broken and her soul was crushed. Her dreams that she had for her son were shattered and worst of all, she knew what would happen to him in prison. That might have been the worst night of her entire life.

She developed and came down with cancer. Some say it was caused by what her son did. She began to lose weight. She was dying. She got extremely sick one day. The son's brother-in-law told him he should stay home. The son chose to keep a date with a girl he was going with. When he did get home his brother-in-law told him to come upstairs where she was quickly fading. His mother had kept asking, "where is my son?" She held onto life until he came. She took his hand and said, "I love you so much." Those were her final words. She died after she said them. Her son had to hear the consequences of what he had done and the pain it had caused. He had to live with this for the rest of his life. He had caused other people some bad pain also. He could not face the regrets of what he had done, especially to his mother. Death must have been a relief to him. His soul had to be affected also. There are moments in our life when we can make a choice. These choices have consequences. We should listen to our conscience which comes from our spirit.

All things come from God. Thank you God for loving and forgiving me. Thank you God for your mercy. I love you dear God.

Love is the Key

Day by day in each and every way, I'm getting better and better, stronger and stronger, through the grace of God.

Love. What a complicated subject. It seems so simple; you love someone or something. There is a little more to it than that. Let's suppose you meet a girl. You fall in "love." You want to be with that person. Eventually your closeness and affection become sexual. The man's hormones take over. He has only one desire and that is to achieve sexual satisfaction. This is not love unless he loves sexual satisfaction. This usually is not love because he has put himself first with little or no respect for the woman. True love would be if he put giving the woman pleasure before he thought of himself. The same holds true for a woman. Another kind of love is a love of things. You cannot love a thing because it is inanimate and has no way to respond. You are basically loving the world and what is in it. You have become more worldly and less spiritual. You can like a thing of the world, but if you love it you are becoming more worldly. True love, unconditional love, is the greatest power in the universe. It holds the universe together.

All things come from God. Thank you God for loving and forgiving me. Thank you God for your mercy. I love you dear God.

Inside You

Day by day in each and every way, I'm getting better and better, stronger and stronger, through the grace of God.

If your life is a room and on all four walls there is nothing but mirrors, all you will ever see is yourself. Your world will be you since you are not able to see beyond yourself. You know there is another world out there, but you can't see it for looking yourself. Time and maturity should allow you to see more than the mirrors, which has covered up a window. When that is uncovered, you can see something other than yourself. The world, your world, will now not revolve around you like it did before. When you look out the window, you may see a crippled man fall. Your mind is now on something besides yourself. As the desire to see more grows, you will have more windows to see the world out of. If you are ever able to take away all of the mirrors, you will be at one with the world. You will be part of the world and all of the people in it. This is a big wide wonderful world if we can only get beyond ourselves. Now that you have experienced the world outside of yourself, you are now ready to experience the world inside of you. Your spirited world will be forever; you can get in touch with your spirited world through God. All things come from God. Once you fully realize this, then you are in a position to become more spiritual. You will experience true humility which fosters love, peace, happiness. The world will have a lot less meaning to you when you become more of a spiritual person, and your spirit will have more meaning.

All things come from God. Thank you God for loving and forgiving me. Thank you God for your mercy. I love you dear God.

Losers

Day by day in each and every way, I'm getting better and better, stronger and stronger, through the grace of God.

We all have heard someone say, "he or she is a loser." They have written that person off. They have lost any respect or regard for that individual. Our judgment can be clouded if we believe what they say. There are a number of reasons this is said of someone. One of the most common is that the person is introverted and appears to have little or no personality. Another reason is a person's lifestyle, which may be unique and does not blend in with the community. The acts that a person has committed such as violence, theft, lack of responsibility regarding money, a spend thrift so to speak. There are other reasons, but it all boils down to the word "loser." God doesn't make losers. There are only people who have not connected to him or those who have not found their purpose in life. Our function as a person who wishes to be spiritual is first to not judge, second to try to see something in this person no one else sees and to accept and encourage them if you come in contact with them. Your spirit will become more highly evolved when you do that.

All things come from God. Thank you God for loving and forgiving me. Thank you God for your mercy. I love you dear God.

To Be or Not to Be

Day by day in each and every way, I'm getting better and better, stronger and stronger, through the grace of God.

"That is the question," said Shakespeare. In our case, it refers to being spiritual or non-spiritual. It all depends which world is most important to you; the world we live in now or the world we will live in the future after we leave this world. We have two natures, our human nature and our spiritual nature. This choice is ours to make as to be more worldly, meaning that possessions, friends, pleasures, dreams, power or a quest to be a superior being will become our passion and will mean almost everything. The other choice is a spiritual person who is humble, loving, patient, and not obsessed with what is in the world we live in now. As stated before, the choice is yours to make. No one can make it for you. It is truly a "to be or not to be" question.

All things come from God. Thank you God for loving and forgiving me. Thank you God for your mercy. I love

you dear God.

Different Direction

Day by day in each and every way, I'm getting better and better, stronger and stronger, through the grace of God.

We are all going in eight different directions. The first direction is the first impression of others and how we react to them and they to us. We will consider them superior, equal or inferior to us. They will do the same. The second involves our interest and goals, which are sincere disciplines such as teachers, either irritable or likeable, actors or performers, either irritable or likeable, and unconcerned dispositions, passive, vacant or happy. The third direction is our home life style, either physical, social, or material. The fourth direction is temperament, which can be unfriendly or friendly, decisive or indecisive, or careful or impulsive. The fifth direction is normal, desirable or neurotic. The sixth direction is the past and how it has affected us. The seventh is the present and how we are dealing with our life on a day-to-day basis. The eighth is the future and what we expect and look forward to. Should we desire to be a spiritual person, then we need to know ourselves before we can know others and be able to accept them on an unconditional basis.

All things come from God. Thank you God for loving and forgiving me. Thank you God for your mercy. I love you dear God.

Something Happens

Day by day in each and every way, I'm getting better and better, stronger and stronger, through the grace of God.

When two people meet for the first time, something happens which neither one of them is aware of, but it determines how the relationship will work out. We have an unconscious habit of putting people in one of three categories which are equal, superior, or inferior to us. The other person does the same thing without realizing it. The relationship is determined by factors neither one is aware of. If someone considers you inferior to them and you consider yourself as their equal, there will be no relationship. If someone considers you equal to them and you feel equal to them, a good relationship is expected. If someone considers you superior then you must recognize this. Give them encouragement and respect and a good relationship. Suppose someone considers you inferior to them, in order to have a relationship with such a person, take a step back and play the role they have assigned to you. If you desire a relationship with them, pay them homage, ask their advice and ask them questions for their opinion. They will still consider you inferior to them, but will say to themselves that you realize that you are inferior or not as good and they will respect that. All of this happens usually in the first 10 minutes of the initial meeting and neither party is aware of what is happening. The spirited person, who has love in his heart will accept the other person no matter how they consider him.

All things come from God. Thank you God for loving and forgiving me. Thank you God for your mercy. I love you dear God.

Judgment

Day by day in each and every way, I'm getting better and better, stronger and stronger, through the grace of God.

Judgment comes in two forms: good and poor. Proper assessment is the vital key to good judgment. The ability to see things for what they are and not what you want them to be is the deciding factor. As to whether your judgment will be good or poor, the greater the person's power and authority is, the more important it is to have good judgment because now their judgment goes far beyond just themselves; it can affect millions of people, as in wars and economic depression. Good judgment depends also on the morality or lack of when judgments are made. If any immoral person makes a decision, it will be based entirely upon what is good for them personally. Others will be of little or no concern. This is why a person, character, and morals should be of the highest concern when deciding which people should be given power over others. Then there is the problem of people

Judgment

sitting in judgment of their fellow man. The ultimate judgment is not for man to make.

All things come from God. Thank you God for loving and forgiving me. Thank you God for your mercy. I love you dear God.

God's Profound Ways

Day by day in each and every way, I'm getting better and better, stronger and stronger, through the grace of God.

He lived a selfish life for decades. He had his good points. He could be kind and generous. He always believed in God ever since he was a small child and looked around and saw trees, plants, and all of nature. He innately believed that humans could not have made all of this natural beauty. There had to be something higher. As he grew, he found out this was God, but that had no relevance to him. He loved life for himself. When he became older, he had an operation that went bad. There were a number of events that led up to that. A series of happenings occurred, which led him to be confined for months on end in a nursing home bed, from which he could not get out of. The only thing he could do was think. He began to think about his life and all the pain he had caused others. He began to ask God to forgive him. He was overwhelmed when it came to him that his life to that point had no meaning. It came to him that he had a purpose. He realized that he had been put in that nursing home bed for a reason. He realized he needed to change and he did. He saw that life is for the spirit and unconditional love. He endured much suffering, but believed that things happen for the best. God sure has a profound way of things working out for the best.

All things come from God. Thank you God for loving and forgiving me. Thank you God for your mercy. I love you dear God.

Users

Day by day in each and every way, I'm getting better and better, stronger and stronger, through the grace of God.

We are all users. We use things for our benefit. We use situations when we can for personal gain. We also use people to work for us, do favors, or perform other functions which we need or want, such as sexual, or for advice or help, or to borrow money from to name just a few. We also use machines to do work for us. We use all types of people and things for our benefit. We are all users, but what kind of users are we? Are we the type of user that when we use something we just throw it away or discard it, even though it has some value? When we use people do we discard them like things when they no longer have a value to us? We take what we can from them, money, sex, or favors and then have nothing more to do with them. People who do this are called "users." They are totally selfish people who have never learned the intrinsic value of other people. When you use people, as you invariably will do, in order to be a more spiritual person, you need to love and value that person. The spiritual person will do that plus they will give more than they get.

All things come from God. Thank you God for loving and forgiving me. Thank you God for your mercy. I love you dear God.

Only God

Day by day in each and every way, I'm getting better and better, stronger and stronger, through the grace of God.

St. Ignatius of Loyola, the founder of the Jesuits, was born in 1491. From early on he was a rascal. He became a womanizer, hellraiser, and someone who cared about nothing or no one, except himself. He became a solider and was seriously injured when a French cannonball went between his legs. He was operated on only to find out that the operation was a failure and his leg had to be broken again. Part of his leg protruded and had to be sawed off. He endured several operations with no painkiller. The pain was unreal. He spent many months in a hospital where he read the lives of the saints. It was during the period of silence, solitude, and pain that he found his spiritual self. He went on to found the Jesuit order, which has thousands of priests, universities, and schools all over the world. The Jesuits have more patents and copyrights than any organization on earth, and now a

Only God

Jesuit is Pope. Something came out of him, his spirit, which we all have. Only God knows what you can do.

All things come from God. Thank you God for loving and forgiving me. Thank you God for your mercy. I love you dear God.

Joy

Day by day in each and every way, I'm getting better and better, stronger and stronger, through the grace of God.

When it comes to joy in our lives, the best we can hope for is sporadic spurts of joy. Of course, some people have more than others. It all greatly depends on what gives us joy. Some people can get joy from the simplest things in life: a beautiful day, a smile from someone you made happy, a cozy room, the touch of someone you love, etc. People who can receive joy from the simple things will always have something to enjoy. People who receive their share of joy in life from acquisition of things or the accomplishments of difficult goals obviously will have less to feel joyful about. The joy experienced by materials and goals will not last very long because of the superficial nature of the source of that joy. Spiritual joy probably comes closest to pure joy since it goes to the inner core of our being and affects our deepest inner feelings. Take the spiritual joy of feeling the presence of God, which will far outweigh any other joy we may experience.

All things come from God. Thank you God for loving and forgiving me. Thank you God for your mercy. I love you dear God.

Peace

Day by day in each and every way, I'm getting better and better, stronger and stronger, through the grace of God.

We live in a world of conflict and strife due to the nature of man and the world in which we live. Man must be, and always will be, a part of this conflict. It is because of this constant conflict going on with nature, others, and even himself that man desires and strives for peace. He desires an absence from conflict with others. Peace is needed to achieve a balance and harmony that will somehow affect the conflict that he knows he will face until his last breath. A person will try to compromise in the interest of peace and may even surrender if it will avoid conflict and lead to peace. In addition to conflict with others, he also has internal conflict. Guilt, hate, envy, neurotic trends, and excessive desires will contribute to internal mental conflict and prevent seeking peace of mind. Peace of mind, however, will not come unless the negative feelings mentioned above

Peace

have been resolved or eliminated. Peace of mind, therefore, is elusive for most people since they wish to hold onto those passions which control them. Peace comes from letting go of worldly desires and concentrating more on the spiritual being within all of us.

All things come from God. Thank you God for loving and forgiving me. Thank you God for your mercy. I love you dear God.

Mercy

Day by day in each and every way, I'm getting better and better, stronger and stronger, through the grace of God.

Mercy can only be given by someone who has power or advantages over another. Perhaps this explains why mercy is in such a short supply. When someone achieves an advantage over another, it's usually so they can take the advantage and take from the other person. This usually being the intent, it would be counterproductive to turn around or relinquish that advantage and have mercy on the one who a person had sought advantage over. The other dispenser of mercy is someone who has power or authority by someone who has no personal connection to the person. Of course, this depends on how the person in power handles power. Somewhere in the giving of mercy, compassion must play a part. Without compassion there can be no mercy granted. Something or someone must touch the heart of the person who is in the position to grant mercy. Compassion can be a

Mercy

permanent or very fleeting, temporary thing, but during the time compassion is felt, the person becomes a better human being. God is the ultimate source of mercy. We have all been a beneficiary of God's mercy whether we know it or not.

All things come from God. Thank you God for loving and forgiving me. Thank you God for your mercy. I love you dear God.

Understanding

Day by day in each and every way, I'm getting better and better, stronger and stronger, through the grace of God.

When someone says of another person, "they understand," it means that the person has a complete idea of the situation or person. A person with understanding not only knows what is really going on, but can see it from all sides. They have the ability to look at things from many different points of view and reserve judgment. Therefore, they are neither critical or judgmental. They are objective and are able to put things and people in perspective without being influenced by personal beliefs or prejudices. They try to understand and do understand a person's side of a situation. They don't take sides and remain neutral, which gives them the ability to see more closely. There is also an element of compassion, mercy, and forgiveness in the person of understanding. It is vital in a relationship that at least one of the partners, preferably both partners, have an understanding nature. The

Understanding

understanding person always remains calm and provides harmony to most situations. A truly understanding person will always be a truly spiritual person.

All things come from God. Thank you God for loving and forgiving me. Thank you God for your mercy. I love you dear God.

Goodness

Day by day in each and every way, I'm getting better and better, stronger and stronger, through the grace of God.

When someone has goodness, true goodness, it comes from the core of their being. It is their essence. The center of them is imbued with a quality that exudes goodness in all situations with all people all of the time. They are constantly good, even in the face of adversity. They do not even think of resorting to vengeance. They are devoid of envy and malice. There is no room in their heart for greed. Hate is a concept that is foreign to them. Lots of people seem to dominate their life. They are able to help those who most people would not. They accept those who most find unacceptable. They basically forgive and hold no grudges. They truly do forgive and even more importantly, they forget. When in their presence you feel a warmth unlike no other. Something in them comes across to you. It can best be described as a warm glow inside of you. When a person with goodness departs this world, people whom they have touched feel like a part of them is missing. When they go, they take away, but they do leave something. A little piece of themselves. Their spirit will always be with those they leave behind.

All things come from God. Thank you God for loving and forgiving me. Thank you God for your mercy. I love you dear God.

Growth

Day by day in each and every way, I'm getting better and better, stronger and stronger, through the grace of God.

Growth normally occurs as a natural process. Physical growth, which does not depend upon the will, usually is not impeded and reaches its full potential. That could be because the organism itself has no control of the process. Mental, emotional, and intellectual growth in the human being is dictated solely by the will of the individual. It is a matter of pure choice. Although some have limited intelligence, they can grow to a greater individual and mental capacity than some with a high degree of intelligence simply because they choose to. Emotional growth is usually thwarted by neurotic tendencies. When we are obsessed with anything it leaves no room for the consideration of others which is probably the basis of all emotional growth. Our basic human instinct to be selfish is the main obstacle to our emotional growth. When we are able to put others at the center of our lives in-

Growth

stead of focusing externally or mostly on ourselves, we begin to put ourselves on the path to true emotional growth. Unlike physical growth this never ends the same as intellectual and mental growth should continue until the end of our lives. Putting others before ourselves will lead to spiritual growth.

All things come from God. Thank you God for loving and forgiving me. Thank you God for your mercy. I love you dear God.

Life

Day by day in each and every way, I'm getting better and better, stronger and stronger, through the grace of God.

When someone is full of life it usually means that they are living life to its fullest. They are expressing the life inside of their body and it's reflected in their life and the way they live. It's not only what you do with your life, it's also what you do with the life that's inside of you. The life inside of you is controlled energy and you are the one that controls it. You can choose to conserve your life or energy force by doing as little as possible or you can use your energy life force to its maximum. Most people lie somewhere between the two. One's lifestyle will also determine how the life energy in your body is used. Excessive eating, sex, alcohol and drugs will drain and deplete your life energy force. Your life and its outcome will greatly depend on the choices you make as to how you will spend the life energy inside of you. A spiritual person will take care of their spirit.

Life

All things come from God. Thank you God for loving and forgiving me. Thank you God for your mercy. I love you dear God.

Alignment

Day by day in each and every way, I'm getting better and better, stronger and stronger, through the grace of God.

Alignment usually refers to cars. They need to be aligned in order to function right. The same holds true when it comes to human beings. People need to keep their priorities straight, that is the arrangement of the most important to come first and the less the importance the lower the rank. A person also needs to have their emotions in line so that emotions do not dominate their thinking and reasoning ability. Values need to also be in a proper order and when values are in line or lined up with their priorities, then like cars, people are able to move ahead unimpeded. Our thoughts also need to be aligned. It is too easy to be preoccupied by too many thoughts at the same time. If our thoughts are arranged in a sequence and processed one by one then the chances of being effective at whatever we do increase greatly. Alignment of thoughts, priorities, values and emotions will keep us on a straight efficient course. Our soul needs a positive unselfish course to be on.

All things come from God. Thank you God for loving and forgiving me. Thank you God for your mercy. I love you dear God.

Spirit

Day by day in each and every way, I'm getting better and better, stronger and stronger, through the grace of God.

Someone who has spirit gives life their all. There is something burning inside of them that takes them further than most people are willing to go. They go over and beyond what is expected. There is another word that means the same as spirit in this context. When someone is said to have "heart" this is a way of saying they have spirit. People who have heart continue on long after everyone else would have given up. They keep on going when a situation appears hopeless. A person's spirit is their essential nature. It's something inside of us that we can't see or feel. The spirit inside of us is our life and depending upon the strength it has determines to a great extent what our life will be like. If we have a weak spirit our effort will usually lack what it takes to be truly successful in any endeavor. Our spirit will always be the best part of us and if we allow ourselves to feel our spirit, life will become more meaningful.

All things come from God. Thank you God for loving and forgiving me. Thank you God for your mercy. I love you dear God.

Radiance

Day by day in each and every way, I'm getting better and better, stronger and stronger, through the grace of God.

There is only one thing that can cause a person to be radiant. Love. Love and only love is the force that emits such joy and happiness that it actually causes a person to be radiant. Love produces a joy within a person that they cannot contain. It will not be encapsulated. It must burst forth. It has created a bolt of energy unlike no other. It is positive, pervasive, and encompassing. It has no limits or boundaries. It transcends all things and captivates even the hardest of hearts. Radiant people are rare and you'll never forget them. They will have impacted you. The purity of their love travels on an energy field that connects all things. You will be affected. The power of this kind of love comes from its purity. It is not contaminated by anything selfish or negative. It is free of self. This is the magic that has been described above as love, a pure love, produced by someone. As wonderful and great as this human love is, if we believe, truly believe in the power of God's love, then it would be no exaggeration to multiply that feeling by a thousand and probably more. The love of a radiant person is the touch of God's love.

All things come from God. Thank you God for loving and forgiving me. Thank you God for your mercy. I love you dear God.

Transcendence

Day by day in each and every way, I'm getting better and better, stronger and stronger, through the grace of God.

Transcendence means that you not only surpass others but that you also surpass yourself, which is even more difficult. Surpassing yourself means that you rise above your own nature and become independent of the material universe, thus inevitably giving greater value to the spiritual and less to the material. When we need and want less of material goods and when we stop devoting ourselves to the accumulation of money and things then we are beginning to transcend over our own nature which is material. When we are able to take pleasure in spiritual experiences rather than pleasures that stimulate our physical body we are on the path to transcendence. When we can put aside negative emotions and think only on the positive, we are taking another step toward transcendence. When we empty our heart of ourselves and let love flow in where only our ego resided before we shall have completed a major step. The physical and material world maintains a strong grip and hold on us. We can transcend but we can never ever tell anyone Humility is the key.

All things come from God. Thank you God for loving and forgiving me. Thank you God for your mercy. I love you dear God.

Beauty

Day by day in each and every way, I'm getting better and better, stronger and stronger, through the grace of God.

Beauty will always be in the eye of the beholder. Beauty is something that is pleasing to the senses and everyone has a different idea of what is pleasing to them, a personal preference so to speak. Beauty in this context usually refers to physical beauty, attractiveness. When a person has beauty as referred to in their character there are other criteria and none of them are physical. When a person is known to have internal beauty, something, that magic something, will come through in their eyes. If the eyes are the mirror of the soul, a person's external beauty will be reflected. Internal beauty is only possible with the absence or negative emotions and feelings. As long as a person harbors a grudge, hate, envy, lust or revenge inside of them, what will be reflected in the eyes will not be beauty. Internal beauty also has a way of manifesting itself in physical beauty. A person

Beauty

can be literally transformed externally when they are transformed internally. True beauty crosses all boundaries. True beauty is beauty of the soul and in the spirit.

All things come from God. Thank you God for loving and forgiving me. Thank you God for your mercy. I love you dear God.

Forgiveness

Day by day in each and every way, I'm getting better and better, stronger and stronger, through the grace of God.

Forgiveness must come straight from the heart. It requires that you renounce all anger and resentment that we previously held. Should the slightest bit remain, then true forgiveness will not take place. It will be only words that have no true meaning. Forgiveness is passing over of offense almost as though it never happened. When you forgive you are saying that you will free the offender from the consequences of their action. When you free them, you are freeing yourself from hatred, resentment and anger. It's as much about freeing yourself as it is the other person or persons. There are those who feel that they do not need your forgiveness, although they really do. It is difficult to forgive those who have expressed absolutely no remorse for what they have done. This is why forgiveness must be done for yourself primarily, since the offender may not want or even need the forgiveness you are offering. In an effort to forgive it's even possible that you will be rejected, ridiculed or even attacked should you go to that person and make your intentions known to forgive them. To err is human, to forgive divine. We are not divine when we forgive, but we are closer to the divine spiritually.

All things come from God. Thank you God for loving and forgiving me. Thank you God for your mercy. I love you dear God.

Opportunity

Day by day in each and every way, I'm getting better and better, stronger and stronger, through the grace of God.

Opportunity is a very fickle phenomenon. Sometimes it comes quickly and sometimes in many varied disguises. Sometimes it creeps upon you and doesn't reveal itself until the last minute. Then there are the opportunities that weren't themselves in neon lights only to disappear unless immediately seized upon. The real talent is recognizing opportunities when they first appear on the horizon. As they move closer and come into plain view, the astute will recognize them and then seize them without hesitation. An opportunity is after all a chance for progress, change or advancement, but it usually only knows one time. If you open the door and let it in your life will change but you, as well, are the door that must be open. If you are closed to the possibility of opportunity and all it possesses you will miss not one but many opportunities both large and small. Opportunities will present themselves in love, business, careers and even health. A person can also create their own opportunities. A life is made up of opportunities both lost and taken. Lost opportunities are sometimes the source of our biggest regrets, especially when God offers you an opportunity to change. You will know when your soul is open to it. Your spirit will tell you.

All things come from God. Thank you God for loving and forgiving me. Thank you God for your mercy. I love you dear God.

Quietness

Day by day in each and every way, I'm getting better and better, stronger and stronger, through the grace of God.

Quietness is the balm of the soul. Silence is necessary for a sane mind and healthy body since it provides the peace and calm, serenity and rest, that allows the body and mind to find its center. Your spirit is silent and it's only when you enter the realm of your spirit that you are able to connect in some small way to the essence of your being. It also operates in silence and communication with the divine is most effective when you enter into God's element., silence. Silence allows your thoughts to be heard for better or worse. It allows our mind to "get things off its chest." Silence gives us the opportunity to come out of ourselves, we can think of others if we so choose. Silence can be our best friend, confidant and spokesman if we only allow it to be; it is also our best connection to our spirit and God.

Quietness

All things come from God. Thank you God for loving and forgiving me. Thank you God for your mercy. I love you God.

Patience

Day by day in each and every way, I'm getting better and better, stronger and stronger, through the grace of God.

Patience is the ultimate in self-control. Patience is being in a very frustrating, irritating situation and dealing with it in a calm, reasonable manner. Patience is thinking and then acting rather than not thinking and reacting. Patience is the intimate expression of love when it involves having it with someone you care about. Patience is putting yourself and your feelings and emotions aside long enough to consider the wisest course of action at the time. Patience is realizing that impatience usually makes the situation worse. Patience is something that you extend to a friend when they have stepped over a line. Patience is more than a virtue, it is an opportunity to be a better person. Patience should be a habit but usually isn't. It is seldom used by some, never by others and most of the time by those who have cultivated patience as a personal habit in their daily life. Patience can become

Patience

elusive depending upon the situation. If we do lose our patience, we have lost the opportunity to be a better person. Patience is letting our soul take over when the human being in us is trying to come out.

All things come from God. Thank you God for loving and forgiving me. Thank you God for your mercy. I love you dear God.

Steadfastness

Day by day in each and every way, I'm getting better and better, stronger and stronger, through the grace of God.

Someone who is steadfast can be depended on, for their behavior is predictable. They have the unique quality of loyalty. They know where they are at, when they are going and how they are going to get there. They are not easily excited or upset due to their stability. A steadfast person usually has been that way for their whole life. They have found that to maintain balance in their life it must possess an unwavering continuous quality. They have confidence not only in themselves but in their position at the present time. A steadfast person usually holds no surprises. People know where he stands and where they stand in relation to that. They also know that he can be depended upon to maintain that position whatever it is. In times of trouble and confusion a steadfast friend is the best friend to have since their moral compass is usually pointing in the right direction. They live according to the direction of their soul and have a spiritual quality.

All things come from God. Thank you God for loving and forgiving me. Thank you God for your mercy. I love you dear God.

Tranquility

Day by day in each and every way, I'm getting better and better, stronger and stronger, through the grace of God.

If there is a road to tranquility it begins with letting go of many things in your life. It means letting go of fear, because it keeps someone in a state of agitation. It means letting go of frustration, since it keeps someone and the people around them tense. Frustration comes from being stymied in getting what you've wanted. Sometimes in order to relieve frustrations you must let go of what you want. This doesn't mean that you quit when you run into obstacles, it means that you continue to work toward what you want, minus the emotion of anger which arises from things not gained the way you feel they should. It means letting go of all negative thoughts and doubts which control your life, your thoughts, your actions and your future. Negative thoughts and feelings will inhibit any chance of tranquility since anxiety will prevail. When we let go of our anxieties, we are letting go of the black cloud which seemed to be following us around, above which is the possibility that something bad will happen, but we don't know where or when. Tranquility can be had but the price is paid in self-control. The soul must be tranquil before we can have true tranquility.

All things come from God. Thank you God for loving and forgiving me. Thank you God for your mercy. I love you dear God.

Greatness

Day by day in each and every way, I'm getting better and better, stronger and stronger, through the grace of God.

Greatness is usually reserved for those who have conquered their own human nature. They have won the biggest battle man will ever have to wage. Most everyone loses the battle with their own nature. They seem to be destined to be victims of themselves. They struggle with ego, pride, greed, lust, envy, arrogance, ignorance, pettiness, vengeance, inferiority, superiority, complacency, powerlessness and most of all, fear. They take the line of least resistance and when they do all of the above, fear descends upon them in a sudden and relentless manner. It does not appear that God created many with the potential for greatness. When the self is overcome it allows the true person to come out and find their destiny. Greatness is not genetic. Kings have proven that over and over. Greatness is acquired usually over a lifetime. Someone who excels in what they do, love and are loved,

Greatness

humble in their victories, courageous and honest, dedicated and with a high standard of morality, have the seeds of
greatness. Greatness, true greatness, is never acknowledged
by those who possess it. Greatness is possessed by the soul.

All things come from God. Thank you God for loving
and forgiving me. Thank you God for your mercy. I love
you dear God.

Wonderment

Day by day in each and every way, I'm getting better and better, stronger and stronger, through the grace of God.

Some people never experience or very seldom have experienced wonderment. They have never been in awe of the wonderful world that surrounds them and which they are a part of. They don't consider anything remarkable. They are never taken by surprise at the range of love that people can be capable of. They have never marveled at the infinite range of plant and animal life and its capabilities. They have not been inspired by the unselfish action of someone who went out of their way to extend themselves to them when they were in need. They have never looked up at the sky and marveled at the vastness of the universe and the fact that the planet they live on not only hangs in space at the same place and that it rotates every 24 hours at exactly the same amount of time to the second or that the sun is the result of the equivalent of a million hydrogen bombs exploding every second. They are not touched by the miracle we call life. Those who do live in wonderment of the world we live in and the power of the God that created it experience life in a dimension and on a plane that fills their life with a far different meaning than others. A spiritual meaning.

All things come from God. Thank you God for loving and forgiving me. Thank you God for your mercy. I love you dear God.

Diversity

Day by day in each and every way, I'm getting better and better, stronger and stronger, through the grace of God.

It sometimes takes courage to do different things in a different way. Diversity is not being afraid to branch out to do something new, exciting and different. The addition of variety to one's life can only enhance it, if the direction is a positive one. There are of course negative paths that one may travel down in the name of diversity. The end of those roads will not be the enhancement of one's life. Diversity can be taken in any number of life's choices. We can become diverse in our career, our hobbies, our finances and friends, and our outlook on life. Diversity is however only beneficial when we have a center in our life and we are grounded as to who we are and our relation to the world and God. Diversity can be accomplished if it has some kind of connection to something that we are familiar with, such as someone who has a successful restaurant may choose to diversify into catering or even producing a food product for distribution in supermarkets. This allows them to maintain their center, which is the restaurant, yet branch out into new and exciting things but with something that is familiar and they are knowledgeable about. We have the ability to diversify into a spiritual meaning for our life.

All things come from God. Thank you God for loving and forgiving me. Thank you God for your mercy. I love you dear God.

Spice

Day by day in each and every way, I'm getting better and better, stronger and stronger, through the grace of God.

Variety is the spice of life, as the old saying goes. This is partially true. Some one can add variety to their life and still be missing the zest that spice is renowned for imparting. Spice in a person's life comes from the daring, the adventurous, the risqué and the different with just a twist. There are a number of reasons why people would like to add a little spice to their life. Spice is known for imparting a zesty flavor to bland food. A person who has decided to spice up their life may in fact have a bland life. Maybe they are bored with a dull, humdrum life that is in a rut going nowhere. Someone who is bored with their life will be a likely candidate to add some zest to their existence. Life's spice may be doing something that you've never done before, or it might be taking a chance or gamble of some sort. It could also be doing something outrageous just for the fun of it or to see

Spice

what happens if you don't. Spice will take you out of the rut that you're in, if you are in fact in a rut. Life's spice is however similar to food spices in the fact that if you add too much you'll ruin it. Perhaps your life will take on a new meaning if you add some spiritual spice to it.

All things come from God. Thank you God for loving and forgiving me. Thank you God for your mercy. I love you dear God.

Potential

Day by day in each and every way, I'm getting better and better, stronger and stronger, through the grace of God.

Mankind's greatest loss is the potential of most people on an individual basis and the loss of potential possessed as a whole by mankind. Very few people ever even come close to the realization of their true potential. Even more people have absolutely no idea what the potential in their lives are. Potential is described as being able to utilize to the maximum the power and talent we possess. Since most people aren't aware of the potential that lies inside of them they of course cannot utilize it fully at all or very seldom. The ability to recognize potential in another person is a great gift only if that person is able to bring out the full potential that rests inside. Hope is one virtue that allows potential to be utilized. Since potential is unrealized possibility, the key ingredient becomes the hope that recognizes the potential and the hope to materialize something that is present but

Potential

does not exist as a fact yet. When someone recognizes potential in another person and tries to give them insight into what is possible in their life, they are helping one human, but in a small way all of mankind. Our greatest potential lies within us, our soul. Faith in our spirit and spiritual life will cause our life to be lived to its fullest potential.

All things come from God. Thank you God for loving and forgiving me. Thank you God for your mercy. I love you dear God.

Ignore

Day by day in each and every way, I'm getting better and better, stronger and stronger, through the grace of God.

Ignore that which you wish to lose and affirm that which you wish to gain. This is not as easy as it sounds. Let's take an ache in your body. You would have to concentrate on having a good or normal feeling where you ache and not pay any attention to the ache. Ignore it. Likewise, we could use the example of a wife or husband who constantly complains about everything. You would have to ignore all the complaining while at the same time affirming how much they have to be thankful for. This requires a great amount of self-control. You must ignore what you wish to lose and affirm that which you will to gain. Simple concept. Difficult to implement. We all have things both within ourselves and others that are hard to ignore much less to say or do something that is affirming about that which you wish to gain. It has to become a habit. You can make the positive outweigh

Ignore

the negative only if you maintain a positive attitude. How do you maintain a positive attitude? You get and maintain a positive attitude when you get a mindset of what is important and what isn't. For example, things of the world are not important compared to things of the spirit. In a short time, things of the world will be gone, nothing will be left. Things of a spiritual nature are infinite. Ignore things of the body and the world. Affirm things of the spirit.

All things come from God. Thank you God for loving and forgiving me. Thank you God for your mercy. I love you dear God.

Gods Way

Heaven never helps the man who will not act.

– Sophocles

Day by day in each and every way, I'm getting better and better, stronger and stronger, through the grace of God.

Some people believe God should do it all. Then they become angry at God when their prayers are not answered or a calamity befalls them. If God had intended for us to be helpless and dependent upon him, he would not have given man a free will and brain. When God created man he intended it to be a partnership. God would supply us with the gifts of life, intelligence and free will. He would also provide us with his own strength when we needed it. We were expected to do the rest. Our job was to use our mind and body to achieve what we needed to accomplish. God did not expect us to just sit back, do nothing and wait for him to solve our problems. We can do most anything with the help of

174

God as long as we help ourselves in the process and do what we can. We would do better to appreciate all that God has given us. If we had this true appreciation, then perhaps we would be more inclined to use God's gifts to help ourselves and do our share as a partner. God has a purpose for us but we must first realize and recognize our spirit side.

All things come from God. Thank you God for loving and forgiving me. Thank you God for your mercy. I love you dear God.

Cervantes

By the streets of "by and by" one arrives at the house of "never."

Day by day in each and every way, I'm getting better and better, stronger and stronger, through the grace of God.

We always seem to be putting off today what we can do tomorrow. Things are somehow expected to be taken care of by and by and some things do. Some things resolve themselves simply through the passing of time, but you can't rely on that. When we expect that, then we will be stranded at the house of never. Things and opportunities will slip through our fingers, never to be come by again. An opportunity lost is more than just an opportunity. It is also the loss of unknown numbers of opportunities that may have resulted from the original opportunity that was lost. We will never know what we missed or what could have been. The cost of procrastination can be higher than we ever imagined due to the unknown resulting losses. Our ability to overcome the natural tendency toward procrastination can be one of our greatest assets. All things are possible but only with the help of God and our spirit.

All things come from God. Thank you God for loving and forgiving me. Thank you God for your mercy. I love you dear God.

Carlyle

Our grand business is not to see what lies dimly at a distance but to do what lies clearly at hand.

Day by day in each and every way, I'm getting better and better, stronger and stronger, through the grace of God.

There are two types of dreamers. There is the dreamer whose dreams are converted into reality through action and then there is the dreamer who does nothing but dream on and on. Dreams without effort to make them come true are like beautiful soap bubbles that float aimlessly in the air. For a few brief moments one can see and admire their beauty but then they vanish into thin air, gone forever. They existed but never became substance. The same holds true for those who are constantly looking into the future forgetting that reality is in the now and present. People whose only dimension is the future overlook the lessons learned from the past and the opportunities presented by the present. The future and the past for all extents and purposes do not exist. They will but the now, the present moment, is really all we have. What we do at this present moment is our life. If we choose to live it in the past or the future, we have wasted it on something that doesn't exist. Spiritual people know and are always looking into their soul for God's guidance.

All things come from God. Thank you God for loving and forgiving me. Thank you God for your mercy. I love you dear God.

Plutarch

The wildest colts make the best horses.

Day by day in each and every way, I'm getting better and better, stronger and stronger, through the grace of God.

Passion cannot be taught or bought. It comes from the care of your being which has been impressed by a combination of ideas and experience. Heart is something you are born with. Either you have it or you don't. Heart being something that keeps you going long past where your body and mind stops. Those who have both passion and heart have spirit. Spirit can be toned down, but never up. Those who have heart, spirit and passion but whose age prevents them from having wisdom sometimes have a tendency to be "wild." There is a natural out for energy that must flow somewhere. After they have obtained some wisdom due to age and experience they tone down somewhat. The energy, spirit, heart and passion are still there but with direction and focus. Intelligence has replaced influence and they direct their vitality into producing constructive goods. Their true potential cannot be denied or limited. Our spirit will guide us if we just let it.

All things come from God. Thank you God for loving and forgiving me. Thank you God for your mercy. I love you dear God.

Wilde

The best way to make children good is to make them happy.

Day by day in each and every way, I'm getting better and better, stronger and stronger, through the grace of God.

Children are happy when they are loved and shown how to love back. Love is easier to teach than might be imagined. People do what makes them feel good and that goes double for kids. When someone loves them and shows it, it makes them feel good and it also makes them feel obligated to do something in return. When you let them give love in return, which is their natural inclination, then it makes them feel even better and happy. When a child is happy then their mind is focused on good things. They don't have a desire to destroy, get back, do mean or say mean things. They are just happy to be who they are and where they are. So many children today are so focused on getting what they want that they end up feeling frustrated when they don't get what they want. Happy kids are happy with what they have. The same holds true with adults. The simple spirit of a child is something to be emulated.

All things come from God. Thank you God for loving and forgiving me. Thank you God for your mercy. I love you dear God.

Montesquieu

The sacred book of the ancient persons says, if you would be holy instruct your children, because all the good acts they perform will be imputed to you.

Day by day in cach and every way, I'm getting better and better, stronger and stronger, through the grace of God.

There is a saying that goes this way: "To teach is to touch a life forever." When we teach our children good values, love and tolerance, courage, honesty, thoughtfulness, consideration and discipline of mind body and spirit, we have imputed not only their physical being, but their soul with the very essence of all that is good in the world and which will go with them into the next and into eternity. What we teach our children, who learn mainly through our own example, will stay with them from then on. This goes for both positive and negative. Our children are a reflection of who we are to a great extent unless they have rejected who and

184

what we are. Someone who leads an exemplary life can also be rejected as well as the deplorable being. We therefore need to go beyond who we are and focus on what our children can be. Should our children find their true God given purpose and spirit, we will have truly been successful as parents.

All things come from God. Thank you God for loving and forgiving me. Thank you God for your mercy. I love you dear God.

Tolstoy

The vocation of every man and woman is to serve other people.

Day by day in each and every way, I'm getting better and better, stronger and stronger, through the grace of God.

Everyone serves somebody no matter who you are. It is the fate of man to be of service to other men. It creates a necessary motion and activity which ensures the process of life. If we are of no service to anyone then we have no purpose in life. Our life will be meaningless. In the matter of money, the more people we serve the more money we make. In the matter of personal satisfaction and happiness, the more people we serve the happier we will be. We as humans need to be of use to someone to be of use to ourselves. If we are to be indispensable, we must be needed because of the service we provide. If companies would adopt a "How can we serve you?" attitude they would possibly find their sales would increase, their employees would have a better morale, their customers would be more loyal and management would be easier. The lack of this attitude can be seen in every area of commerce. It makes the difference between excellence and mediocrity. Spiritual people go beyond service. They love and serve.

All things come from God. Thank you God for loving and forgiving me. Thank you God for your mercy. I love you dear God.

B.C. Brodie

Nothing in the world is so good as usefulness. It binds your fellow creatures to you and you to them. It tends to the improvement of your own character and gives you a real importance in society much beyond what any artificial station can bestow.

Day by day in each and every way, I'm getting better and better, stronger and stronger, through the grace of God.

To be a useful person is one of life's greatest causes. A useless person is really needed by no one simply because they are of no use to anyone including themselves. It can be a mystery as to how they arrived at that state and perhaps if we knew how people degenerate into a useless state, we could do something to keep it from happening. In the long run, however, it usually still comes down to a series of choices that a person makes in the process of becoming useless. They can choose to do nothing as opposed to doing something. They can choose to help themselves as opposed

188

to not helping themselves. There are only a few of the major choices that are made on the road to becoming useless and once a person is useless, they feel useless or they feel useless and so become useless. Either way it is one of life's greatest tragedies. The spiritual person will always find a use for their life.

All things come from God. Thank you God for loving and forgiving me. Thank you God for your mercy. I love you dear God.

Horace

Ridicule is frequently employed with more power and success than severity.

Day by day in each and every way, I'm getting better and better, stronger and stronger, through the grace of God.

Even in ancient times ridicule was known to be the most potent of weapons, stronger sometimes than brute force, for it attacks the core of the man or men. If you want to make an enemy for life, use a combination of ridicule and humiliation. The power of these two combines to have such a devastating effect on someone that it triggers a very basic instinct to not only get even but to destroy those who would do it. Ridicule by itself will render a person and their beliefs and position to being a joke and as such provokes laughter. And laughter at a person renders them completely defenseless and humiliated. When we can make fun of someone or something with an element of truth to it, it has the power far beyond any severe action that can be taken. A severe action and its effect will pass over time. The impact of ridicule is branded into the mind and inner being. It will never stop festering. We know what ridicule and humiliation does. We should consider what effect its opposite, encouragement, can have on the human spirit. The more humble we can become the more spirited we can become and the greater impact our words of encouragement will be.

All things come from God. Thank you God for loving and forgiving me. Thank you God for your mercy. I love you dear God.

Emerson

Whoso would be a man must be a non-conformist.

Day by day in each and every way, I'm getting better and better, stronger and stronger, through the grace of God.

A man can only be a man if he knows who he is and what he is. This means that sometimes what he believes or how what he decides to do may not conform to what is popular. He may go against the majority and become a minority of one in a small group. This takes courage, to stand up against everyone who sees things differently. It can involve being rejected and even humiliated and ridiculed. To stand up in the face of these things requires character that most people probably don't have. The majority of people will go along to get along. It's the lazy and safe way out, but in the process, they lose part of themselves. They give away part of who they are to the mentality of the majority and realize they are only a small part of the majority. They become a smaller person with less of an identity. This identity becomes the identity of the majority. A man who refuses to conform to the majority retains his own identity. Each of us has an identity, a purpose, and a soul. These three things belong to us and not the majority.

All things come from God. Thank you God for loving and forgiving me. Thank you God for your mercy. I love you dear God.

What Are You Looking for?

All of us have two natures. The physical and the spiritual. Our physical side, which is our body, is the most amazing thing in this world. God has given us this remarkable body, which is so complex, it is still not fully understood. God has also given us almost unlimited intelligence and we only use less than 1% of it. Best of all, God has given us choice. We are free to choose what we will do and what we will think. God has also given us time. We have years, months, days, hours, and seconds before we expire.

God has also given us a wonderful world in which to live with beautiful plants and flowers, animals of all kinds, mountains, rivers, streams, oceans, and all of the magnificent things of nature. However, God has given us the greatest gift of all, a spirit which is infinite. We can choose to be worldly or spiritual. We will die and everything in the world will disintegrate, including the world itself. Our spirit will not die. If you are looking for true peace, joy, and happiness, it can be found in the spirit, not in the world.

Your choice.

Choice

Day by day in each and every way, I'm getting better and better, stronger and stronger, through the grace of God.

Everything is a choice. We think thousands of thoughts and out of these thoughts come choices. We can be thinking about two opposing things, but we will choose one over the other. We choose to do everything we do. When someone says, "I didn't mean to do that." I'm sorry but you did mean to do it because you chose. To Along with freedom to choose comes responsibility. We are responsible for what we do. No one else is. It's on us. The best part of choice is that if we· decide that we want to become more spiritual, we can choose to put God above the world and put God before ourselves, and the choices become easier. If you truly are becoming more spiritual, God will talk with you and tell you what to do. You just have to listen for God so you can make the right choices. The choice is yours.

Choice

All things come from God. Thank you God for loving and forgiving me. Thank you God for your mercy. I love you dear God.

Spiritual Maturity

Day by day in each and every way, I'm getting better and better, stronger and stronger, through the grace of God.

We as human beings never stand still. We are either going forward or backward. When we are stagnant, it creates the illusion we are not moving or losing momentum, but we are. The human being was designed to grow and mature, not to stagnate and digress. Growth comes from a choice to increase our capacity and develop our natural talents and abilities. If we choose to do nothing, then we choose to go backward, as in a backward person. Growth of all kinds is the key to our maturity. Some of the things that are meant for growth are of a spiritual nature. We also need to grow emotionally and intellectually. The growth of empathy toward our fellow man is probably one of the most important areas in which we need to grow. Our spiritual growth is contingent upon the growth of our outlook on God and the world. Our growth should only end with the last breath we take. Those among us who choose to grow are more of an inspiration to others than they realize.

All things come from God. Thank you God for loving and forgiving me. Thank you God for your mercy. I love you dear God.

Spiritual Growth

Day by day in each and every way, I'm getting better and better, stronger and stronger, through the grace of God.

Our spirited growth begins with our emotional growth. If we are unable to grow emotionally or control our basic nature, then we have no chance of ever experiencing spiritual growth. Spiritual growth begins with absolute humility and the realization that we are less. The next step is to develop an intense desire to know and become close and part of the divine power that was responsible for our creation. Our quest will be lost if we have expectations. We must expect nothing if we wish to grow spiritually. Our desire to have will distance us from the divine. Those who are willing to give all and who do not wish, desire or expect anything will experience true spiritual growth. Spiritual growth is the hardest of all growths since it must defy and overcome our basic human nature to satisfy ourselves in some way. The nature of spirit is at the same time nothing and everything.

200

Spiritual Growth

All things come from God. Thank you God for loving and forgiving me. Thank you God for your mercy. I love you dear God.

Awe

Day by day in each and every way, I'm getting better and better, stronger and stronger, through the grace of God.

If someone is in awe of someone or something on this earth, the chances are that they are insecure or feel inadequate or inferior. There is really nothing on this earth that should inspire that kind of wonder, veneration or reverence. The person who knows who he is stands in awe when he looks at the shine on a star lit night and realizes that each one of those stars in the sky is like our own sun. He also stands in awe when a flower blooms or an ant carrying ten times its weight across the floor, or a bee hovers in midair in one place, a feat that human engineers say is impossible, yet there it is. The person who has the clarification of awe will be inspired by the magnificence of what God has created and the life he has been given. The person who lives in awe is truly humbled by the miracle of life that he sees every day, realizing that he is part of a great plan, although he doesn't understand it. Awe should be exclusively revered and cherished.

All things come from God. Thank you God for loving and forgiving me. Thank you God for your mercy. I love you dear God.

Fulfillment

Day by day in each and every way, I'm getting better and better, stronger and stronger, through the grace of God.

What does it take to be fulfilled as a person? This of course depends on the person. What will fulfill one person will not fulfill the next. Fulfillment is usually conceived in a very positive way. It is almost never thought of in a negative context. This is probably because when a person is fulfilled, they are complete and satisfied. When someone indulges in negative, destructive goals, they will never be complete. An example is the child molester. He can never feel satisfied, much less complete as a person. There will always be something missing in his life. This being said, it can also probably be said that not too many people are fulfilled as human beings. There always seems to be something missing in their life. A life devoted to materials and pleasure will usually always be wanting because it cannot seem to ever be satisfied with enough or sated with pleasure. Until the

Fulfillment

spiritual part of us is complete or satisfied, we will never be fulfilled. It takes something of a spiritual nature to complete us and lead us to fulfillment.

All things come from God. Thank you God for loving and forgiving me. Thank you God for your mercy. I love you dear God.

Brotherhood

Day by day in each and every way, I'm getting better and better, stronger and stronger, through the grace of God.

"We are all brothers under the skin," so the saying goes. When you take away the skin, we all look the same. There is no difference; since there is no difference, we all have the same thing in common. We are all united and form a common bond of humanity. The humanity God created was when he made us all "brothers under the skin." Besides being united by having a common existence, we are all united in the fact that we have a soul. We have a thread of God running through us that connects us all to one another, whoever and wherever we are. We are truly the brotherhood of many. Since we all are so connected, it is only logical to assume that what happens to one, has an effect of some kind on all of us. Negative and positive. Both run the same way. When we commit a negative act on one of our brothers, we commit it on all. Brotherhood is realizing that we have an obligation to treat our brothers in a positive way for the benefit of all, including ourselves, because it will eventually come back to us since we are all connected.

All things come from God. Thank you God for loving and forgiving me. Thank you God for your mercy. I love you dear God.

Wisdom

Day by day in each and every way, I'm getting better and better, stronger and stronger, through the grace of God.

What price is wisdom? The cost of wisdom bears a high price tag, but it can't be bought by ordinary means. One of the prices of wisdom is pain. The pain of misguided actions resulting in suffering for those making the mistake, and for those who suffer because of the mistake made by another person. A person who will eventually obtain wisdom will be affected by their personal suffering and of those they caused to suffer. If they feel nothing for the other person, their egotistic personality will prevent them from gaining wisdom from the experience. A wise person will make many mistakes before they are able to discern what is lasting, true and right. These mistakes can be and usually are costly. There is no easy way to gain wisdom. A person who does nothing and takes no chances will never gain wisdom. It is reserved for those who can distill what is real from unreal, true from false, and valid or invalid. This takes a lot of years. It is not an overnight epiphany sort of thing. The reward of wisdom is common sense and good judgement, as well as a balanced perspective. The truly wise person will never ever claim they have wisdom. Claiming you have wisdom is the ultimate proof that you don't have it and probably don't even know what it means. People of wisdom realize it is a hard-won gift which needs no recognition of it to exist. God is the source of all wisdom.

All things come from God. Thank you God for loving and forgiving me. Thank you God for your mercy. I love you dear God.

Strength

Day by day in each and every way, I'm getting better and better, stronger and stronger, through the grace of God.

"God give me the strength to . . ."

This sentence is usually finished by an object that the strength is needed for, whatever that is, even if it's only to endure what seems unendurable. Strength is the power to resist forces that are exerted upon us. We as human beings will always have to deal with the laws of nature, where the internal mechanisms result in conflict of one kind or another. We need our greatest strength to deal with the battles which rage within us. We will always be in conflict with ourselves, and our greatest victories will always be when we can overcome our own nature, which is exerting constant pressure upon us to accommodate the needs and wants of our being. Firmness of will, character, mind, and purpose are the necessary attributes if we are to succeed in the battle to conquer ourselves. We also need moral courage too, and

Strength

the power to resist the temptations that the forces of nature constantly assail us with. Our strength comes from within and from the greatest source of power and strength—God.

All things come from God. Thank you God for loving and forgiving me. Thank you God for your mercy. I love you dear God.

Power

Day by day in each and every way, I'm getting better and better, stronger and stronger, through the grace of God.

Power corrupts and absolute power corrupts absolutely. There is truth in this statement: Power is one of the things that people will fight, sometimes to the death, to keep. The power of power is that it gives a person control over others and/or situations. It is the epitome of temporary security. The reality is that it is temporary, but those who have it see it only as absolute. It makes them soft; it makes them secure. It puts them superiors to others. It, in a word, achieves all the things their human nature strives for. Recognition, a feeling of importance, the ability to consummate their desires for things that they want like sex, pleasure, materials, goods, etc….. Power equals control. Power equals great influence and the ability to influence based on the power they have. Power is authority. Power corrupts because the desires of the human being can never be sated. When the power to take is granted, there is no such thing as enough. Continual taking turns into absolute greed and hurt, which destroys the essence of the soul and connection to God.

All things come from God. Thank you God for loving and forgiving me. Thank you God for your mercy. I love you dear God.

Our Nature

Day by day in each and every way, I'm getting better and better, stronger and stronger, through the grace of God.

The nature of the world we live in produces conflict, which in turn causes stress. The world in which we live is in a constant state of change, which also produces stress. The natural basis of our material world, because it is material of matter and energy, is comprised of two opposing forces, which is the cause of all conflict and change. These two forces are opposition and proposition. When something of matter exists or is proposed to exist, it is automatically challenged by an opposing force. This can be seen in the behavior of atoms, the smallest to the largest of galaxies. The minute something is born or created, forces are brought into play to bring about its death or demise. There is a time to be born and a time to die. The two opposing forces and their conflict consume the time between. The human being is in the middle and part of this struggle. Not only is the human being around the relentless forces of nature and other people, the human being is also the victim of internal forces within themselves. This never-ending struggle and conflict with nature, people, and themselves is what life is made of. You have a physical nature and a spiritual nature. The physical has an ending in death. The spiritual is infinite.

All things come from God. Thank you God for loving and forgiving me. Thank you God for your mercy. I love you dear God.

Training

Day by day in each and every way, I'm getting better and better, stronger and stronger, through the grace of God.

With the proper training, a person can be capable of almost anything. All training is beneficial in one way or another. It can be said that there is only one type of training and that is auto training or training of yourself. Others can try to train you, but only you can train yourself to become proficient with practice. Others may be needed to influence you, but only you can practice to become better at it. You can train yourself to do almost anything: get up at a set time each morning without an alarm clock, keep your temper in check, look at the right bright side, and so on. Training yourself usually refers to training yourself to do positive things, but you can train to do negative things, like lie with a straight face, force other people suggestions, or even train to kill. Whatever the training, the person who has it and does it is the most proficient. One form of training that is prob-

216

Training

ably the most beneficial of all is spiritual training—training yourself to get in touch with your spiritual side through God.

All things come from God. Thank you God for loving and forgiving me. Thank you God for your mercy. I love you dear God.

Holiness

Day by day in each and every way, I'm getting better and better, stronger and stronger, through the grace of God.

Some people are regarded rightly or wrongly, as "holier than thou." This usually refers to people who try to give the impression that they are of a higher moral standard than most people. In their attempt to be "holier than thou" they actually can be less moral since their holiness reveals the sin of pride; thus, those who are considered "holier" are belittled in that fashion because they will not violate their moral code or belief when others around them are behaving immorally. This takes a lot of courage to stand up for what you feel is right in the face of many who behave in the opposite. A person of holiness strives to have virtue, which they have faith that it can be gained or derived from a divine being. They desire to live their life according to a higher moral code based on spiritual principles of love, honor, and a firm belief in the divine power of God. When a life is truly lived according to these precepts, it takes strong and deep faith in God to adhere to.

All things come from God. Thank you God for loving and forgiving me. Thank you God for your mercy. I love you dear God.

Righteousness

Day by day in each and every way, I'm getting better and better, stronger and stronger, through the grace of God.

A righteous person does what is within his power to make things right, not only with humility but with others. He continually strives to meet the standards of what is just for all. There is no question of compromise when it comes to the right thing to do or the right way to be. He is dedicated to all that is authentic and true. He is true to his beliefs and connections. A truly righteous person violates no one. We are always faced with choices, which will usually include the intellectual or smart choice, and the right choice. Sometimes they are the same, but not always. The intellectual thing to do will benefit us, but at what expense to another? The right thing may case us pain and hardship, but we cannot escape the fact that it is the right thing to do, even if we choose not to do the right thing. The righteous person who is truly righteous feels he has no choice except to do the right thing. Truly righteous people are rare and spiritual.

All things come from God. Thank you God for loving and forgiving me. Thank you God for your mercy. I love you dear God.

Awareness

Day by day in each and every way, I'm getting better and better, stronger and stronger, through the grace of God.

Awareness requires a constant vigilance. To be aware, someone must always be watchful of the things going on around him in his world, and in the world in general. Someone must be alert to things which seem to have no meaning, realizing that everything and everyone has meaning. This is because everything and everyone is connected, and what affects one thing, affects everything, and what affects one person, affects everyone in some way. Awareness means being mentally alert to what is going on inside of us. What is calling us to do the things we do or say the things we say? Introspection of awareness will reveal things that we prefer not to be aware of. Awareness is created by the desire to know—to know our world, the world generally, and most of all ourselves because until we are aware of ourselves, we will not be truly aware of anything since we are connected to everything and everybody. This is a spiritual connection within us.

All things come from God. Thank you God for loving and forgiving me. Thank you God for your mercy. I love you dear God.

Loveliness

Day by day in each and every way, I'm getting better and better, stronger and stronger, through the grace of God.

Loveliness can refer to someone who has love in his or her heart. In fact, it usually means that they are full of love. So full in fact, that they inspire love and affection in others, and touch the hearts of those around them. Their being is love predominate, and they have pleasing and attractive qualities because of this. They are truly enjoyable and delightful to be around; they are open to people and unafraid to let people into their heart. Their kind of love asks nothing in return, but is given freely with no expectation of receiving something in return. People who have the quality of loveliness forgive easily and hold no grudges. There is no room in their heart for revenge. Their love prevents them from saying anything bad or negative of another person. Most of us only meet a very few of these people in our whole lifetime. They are very special people and when you meet one you will never forget them. You have met a truly spiritual person.

All things come from God. Thank you God for loving and forgiving me. Thank you God for your mercy. I love you dear God.

Serenity

Day by day in each and every way, I'm getting better and better, stronger and stronger, through the grace of God.

Serenity is not a gift; it is not inherited either. It is won. It is acquired by ignoring the things and people in life who are at odds with themselves and everyone. It involves observation of situations and people along with a deep understanding of both. It requires total introspection as to how we react to situations and others. After this has all been determined, in a thorough objective way, then a determination is made not to let happenings, situations, and people disturb our outlook on life, which is positive. It becomes necessary to "let go" of fear, anger, revenge, jealousy, hate, greed, lust, and all other negative desires. When someone "lets go" of the negative elements in their life, it is replaced by positive experiences, which have a calming effect along with a sense of elation. The determination not to let anything or anybody disturb your peace of mind requires more discipline than most people are capable of enacting or even choosing to enact. The person who has captured serenity is a walking example of someone who is in touch with their spirit.

All things come from God. Thank you God for loving and forgiving me. Thank you God for your mercy. I love you dear God.

Guidance

Day by day in each and every way, I'm getting better and better, stronger and stronger, through the grace of God.

Guidance must always come from one of two sources and sometimes both. External guidance comes from others, be they family, friends, or people who are paid to counsel and guide. As with everything, there is a plus and minus side. On the plus side, others can be more objective and less emotionally involved than the person they are advising. On the minus side, they can only imagine what the person is feeling and more importantly, how they are affected by these feelings. They can never truly walk in that person's shoes. The guidance we receive internally will always be distorted by emotions, beliefs (sometimes false) and personal survival instincts. We are likely to fall victim to our personal prejudices and will also have a tendency to compensate for our own character flaws and failings. On the plus side, if we are able to be absolutely honest with ourselves, there should be

Guidance

no one who knows us better than we do. The guidance we receive especially in youth will determine this course of our life. Our best guidance will come from God if we choose to have a spiritual nature.

All things come from God. Thank you God for loving and forgiving me. Thank you God for your mercy. I love you dear God.

Everyone

This book is written for everyone because everyone has a soul, and just as the body needs nourishment, the spirit also needs some spiritual nourishment especially those who are in "low spirits." Hopefully, this little book will not only give you that nourishment, but a positive feeling about your life and yourself. We are all destined to go to another world: the spirit world. This book does not presume to know what is on the other side, but it would seem that if your spirit is filled with the love of God, love for others, and kindness of heart, those will be a big plus on the other side.

Summation

By now, you are hopefully aware that the things of this world are unimportant when they are compared to the spiritual. You are also hopefully aware that this physical shell called our body has almost no relevance when compared to our spirit, which is eternal and infinite. It is hoped that you have been helped in some small way to become more spiritual. If you have been helped to become more spiritual, even in just one way, then the purpose and goal of this book will have succeeded.

God bless you and most of all, God bless your spirit.

www.ingramcontent.com/pod-product-compliance
Lightning Source LLC
Chambersburg PA
CBHW031544040426

42452CB00006B/183